"This is no ordinary book about money ... life experiences of a couple who have ... finances and survived."

> —Chuck Thompson
> Editor, Crown Financial Ministries

"I've had the great privilege to know Marybeth and Curt for years and I can say firsthand that they live what they teach. If you apply the principles of this book, you will have a greater peace about your finances, develop a plan to get out and stay out of debt, and understand how to make your money work for you rather than against you. I give this book my highest endorsement."

> —Lysa TerKeurst
> President, Proverbs 31 Ministries and best-selling author

"Marybeth and Curt have been there. They have walked a path of financial bondage, only to decide to tackle the problem together and walk the painful but gratifying road of becoming debt free. Their heart is to help you change not only your financial situation, but also your marriage in the midst of that stress. Woven with true-to-life stories that hit home, *Learning to Live Financially Free* is a needed book for today's money-strapped couples."

> —Mary DeMuth
> Author, *Authentic Parenting in a Postmodern Culture*

LEARNING TO LIVE
FINANCIALLY
free

Hard-Earned
Wisdom for Saving
Your Marriage &
Your Money

MARYBETH WHALEN & CURT WHALEN

Kregel
Publications

Learning to Live Financially Free: Hard-Earned Wisdom for Saving Your Marriage & Your Money

© 2009 by Marybeth Whalen and Curt Whalen

Published by Kregel Publications, a division of Kregel, Inc., P.O. Box 2607, Grand Rapids, MI 49501.

ISBN 978-0-8254-4188-2

Printed in the United States of America

09 10 11 12 13 / 5 4 3 2 1

To our six wonderful, unique children.
You are a blessing from God.
Jack, Ashleigh, Matthew, Rebekah, Bradley, and Annaliese,
thank you for your patience as we learned how to manage
money and for the sacrifices you were willing to make.
We pray that watching us learn the hard way has
made you wiser and will bless your financial futures.

*Character is following through
on a good decision after
the excitement of making the
decision has passed.*
—KEN BLANCHARD

CONTENTS

ACKNOWLEDGMENTS

To the One who always does more than we can ask or imagine. This book is just another example of that.

To our agent, Bill Jensen, thank you for championing this book and helping shape it into what it has become. Your input has been invaluable.

To the staff of Kregel Publications, thank you for having a vision for the need for this book. It is an honor to work with you.

To our parents, Jay and Sandy Brown, Trudy and Richard Griffin, and Curtis and Betty Whalen, you have helped us in countless big and little ways through the years. Your continued love and support is a great blessing to us.

To our siblings, Becky, Rohn, Mark, Sharon, and Jennifer. Some of your stories are shared here and are, always, woven into ours.

To Sybil and Herb Tillman, thanks for opening your beautiful home to us.

To our church staff and all the volunteers at Elevation, thank you for making church a place we love coming to every week.

To Crown Financial Ministries and Dave Ramsey's organization, without these two groups' materials, our family would not be where we are today. Thank you for all you do.

To Chuck Thompson, editor of Crown's *Money Matters* newsletter, thank you for first publishing our writing and helping us realize we had a story to tell.

ACKNOWLEDGMENTS

To our friends, old and new, who have supported us and lent your stories to this book, and especially to the people who pitched in and surprised us with an extreme home makeover, most notably the Fergusons, the Marsdens, the Cianciosas, and the Frees. We will never forget your generosity.

To the team at Proverbs 31 Ministries, you are more than just people we do ministry with, you are all family.

Chapter 1

FINDING HOPE

Marybeth

Several years ago, my husband, Curt, and I traveled to Florida to visit my stepsister, Becky, and her husband, Chuck. Curt and I enjoyed a few days away from our kids and reconnected with family members we don't get to see very often. One evening the four adults snuck away for a nice, leisurely dinner at Wolfgang Puck's at Pleasure Island in Disney World. The environment was festive and fun, and all of our spirits were light as we sat around the table enjoying the sights, sounds, and delicious smells.

At one point during the conversation, we got on the subject of struggles we'd experienced in marriage. Curious as to the low points of other couples (we've certainly had our share!), I asked Becky and Chuck what their lowest point had been. Without even pondering, Becky blurted out, "When we didn't have any money. Chuck had just taken a job and wasn't making much as a starting salary. I can clearly remember one time when I went to the grocery store and my card was declined because it was maxed out. I'll never forget having to leave my groceries behind. I felt like every eye in the store was watching me. That was the scariest point in the history of our marriage—and it took awhile for it to get better."

Becky and Chuck's financial situation did change. They reached a place of financial comfort and their marriage survived that difficult time. Yet as they sat at dinner that night—years after that difficult time—Becky could easily recall the fear of struggling with money. That period still counted as the roughest trouble they had ever faced—beyond other family issues, several cross-country moves, and even some health problems. Not having enough money and struggling to pay for basic needs had left an indelible mark on their marriage.

I never forgot that moment with Becky and Chuck. I think of it often, as it is a telling commentary on the power that financial issues can have in a marriage. Marriages break up every day over money. Mismanagement, miscommunication, and misunderstandings drive a wedge between husband and wife. Instead of getting in the ring and fighting for their finances together, many couples throw their hands up and walk away—from the problems, but also from each other. In a study done by *Money* magazine, 84 percent of those surveyed said that money causes tension in their marriage, and 13 percent said they fight about money several times a month.[1] Another study cited that 37 percent of couples say that debt is the number one issue that will spark a fight. "Numerous studies have shown that money is the number one reason why couples argue—and many of the recently divorced say those battles were the main reason why they untied the knot."[2]

Curt and I teetered on the edge of throwing in the towel on our marriage many times. We'll tell our story throughout this book, and we'll also share the lessons we learned during our time in the ring as we literally fought to get our finances under control. Our prayer is that this book will help other couples find the freedom that can result from living financially sound lives. The truth is, money is not an isolated issue within a marriage—it infiltrates every other area of the marriage. From the kitchen to the bedroom, money problems will follow you. Once you get a handle on this area of your marriage, you'll find that other problems seem to evaporate into thin air. It's been our experience that the stress of money problems adds an air of negativity to the marriage as a whole. Working together to eliminate those problems can breathe fresh hope and life into what seemed like a lifeless, hopeless situation.

If you've picked up this book, then chances are you need to make some changes in your finances. And you're not alone. Our country as a whole is in a downward financial spiral that is picking up speed with each turn of the calendar page. "On average, today's consumer has a total of 13 credit obligations on record at a credit bureau. These include credit cards (such as department store charge cards, gas cards, or bank cards) and installment loans (auto loans, mortgage loans, student loans, etc.). Of these thirteen credit obligations, nine are likely to be credit cards and four are likely to be installment loans."[3] "Revolving consumer debt, almost all from credit cards, now totals $957 billion, compared with $800 billion in 2004, according to the Federal Reserve. Average car loans are up, too, to $27,397, from $24,888 four years ago. Home mortgages total $10.5 trillion, compared with $7.8 trillion in 2004."[4]

Our personal financial choices are now being reflected on a national level. As we write these words, our nation is experiencing one of the hardest economic challenges since the Great Depression. For decades we have lived beyond our means, using debt as a tool to obtain our wants. And now our house of cards is crumbling around us. We find ourselves with a national debt that has surpassed the ten-trillion-dollar mark, a banking system that is undergoing radical change, and billions of dollars of value that has been lost on Wall Street as the Dow plummets from over 14,000 down to lows we never thought possible. Economists have stopped asking if we're going to be in a recession and started asking how bad and how long it will be.

The national climate of anxiety and uncertainty is also the climate of many homes.

A Commitment to Change

The reality of our poor financial choices hit Curt and I one night four years ago, a few days before Christmas. What should have been a time of festivities and celebrating became just another cause for stress. We didn't know how we were going to afford the expensive presents on the kids' lists. We didn't want to tell them *no*, yet to buy gifts meant adding to our already overwhelming debt load. Because of our faith, we took God at His word when He said that nothing is impossible with Him (Luke 1:37). And yet, from where we sat, our situation looked impossible.

For years, we'd been trying to do something to change our financial picture, to no avail. We desperately wanted to stop using credit cards, yet financial emergencies always cropped up that drove us back to credit card purchases. We wanted to begin tithing and saving, yet there was never any money left over to do that. We wanted to begin chipping away at our debt, and yet we saw no way to do so. We felt trapped at every turn. We'd gotten ourselves into a financial mess. Never before that night had we felt more strongly about getting out of our mess.

As we sat in our parked car at a shopping center near our home. I watched as the other shoppers bustled past us, intent on their lists and last minute errands. I vaguely wondered how many of them were slipping deeper into debt as they charged purchases they couldn't really afford. Meanwhile, Curt and I talked for over an hour, working through what it would take for us to change our spending habits and take steps toward achieving our dream of being debt free. Though neither of us realized it yet, that night was the beginning of a major change in our lives. We were embarking on a journey that would enable us to escape the bondage of debt and begin to enjoy financial freedom. It would be a journey of many years as we endeavored to live differently from the rest of the culture and swim against the current on money issues.

I've often wondered why that night was different than our many other conversations throughout our marriage that had begun, "What are we going to do about our money problems?" Although some of our past efforts had resulted in temporary changes, nothing we did ever stuck. We quickly slipped back into our old ways and debt always seemed to creep back in. Even if we closed a door, debt seemed to find a window. So what made this night—this conversation—different?

First, just a few days before, we'd learned we were expecting a baby. This news had prompted us to evaluate how we could become more financially stable as we prepared for this additional responsibility. In short, it was time to get serious. Second, this impending life change and the urgency we both felt resulted in a unity of purpose that we'd never had before. In the past, our convictions about getting out of debt and making hard changes were usually separate, with one person not as sold on the necessity of the plan. We had never been on board at the same time.

Finally, and most importantly, God met with us that night in the car, allowing Curt and me to feel the same conviction and urgency. God went before us and prepared our hearts, as He is faithful to do. We looked across that car at each other and decided that, not only *could* we do this, but that together we *would* do this. Whatever it took. In our ignorance we were actually excited about working together to slay this debt monster and change our financial picture. God created unity where once there had been anger and blaming.

Heart Attitudes

Since that night, I've learned that getting out of debt requires allowing several basic attitudes to take root in our hearts. Notice I did not say in our minds. The Bible points to the heart as the center—the very essence—of who we are. Proverbs 4:23 says, "Above all else, guard your heart, for it is the wellspring of life." All of our thoughts and actions flow from our hearts. It's funny how we seem to relate money to our heads and not our hearts. But we miss the mark when we do that. Without allowing these attitudes to take root in our hearts—at the very center of our being—our plan for debt reduction would have quickly fallen by the wayside as unexpected expenses and "opportunities" came our way. By presenting a united front in our battle with debt and allowing these attitudes to determine our actions, we've been able to stick with our plan. Though we'll go into the specifics of our plan in other chapters, I first want to cover these four heart attitudes.

An Attitude of Commitment

Because we saw the necessity of reducing our debt and were committed in our hearts to doing that at all costs, we were not tossed about by the waves (Eph. 4:14) when real life hit. We set a goal and held each other accountable to reaching that goal. We are committed to God and to each other as a team. Our plan to become debt free was a long-range plan. In a world of fast food, microwaves, and instant access, it's not easy to walk out every agonizing step in a long-range plan. We knew that results would be long in coming and that we had to fix our eyes on the goal, not the circumstances, and hang onto the Lord to get us through. We'll spend all of chapter 4 talking about how to become a team.

An Attitude of Obedience

A key to obedience is recognizing God's ownership of all things. We were both convinced that God would help us get out of debt if we were obedient to Him. This obedience required me especially to obey not only God, but my husband as well. Though submission is a dirty word in most circles, it was essential on our journey. I had to let my husband lead—even when I doubted his decision and even when he made mistakes. I couldn't step out of the chain of command, and at first I had to continually confess this struggle to the Lord. The good news is, it got easier for me, and my husband became a natural leader for our family. The more power I handed over to him, the more I saw him grow. I am the direct beneficiary of the blessings of obedience. Through this journey, I've had many opportunities to show my husband my respect, trust, and honor as our provider and leader of our home.

An Attitude of Surrender

This period of getting out of debt hasn't been all rosy, as we'll relate later in this book. Obedience has required sacrifice. I've had to surrender my wants and reduce my expectations. I've had to learn to go without, to trust God to provide, and to lay down my desires. We've both had to make adjustments in our spending and truly "count the cost" of every spending decision. We've learned to surrender our desires in the name of honoring God's plans for our family, trusting Him to continually bring about the best outcome possible—more than we can ask or imagine (Eph. 3:20).

An Attitude of Prayer

As we've laid down our wants, we've had to go to God and cast all our anxiety on Him (1 Peter 5:7). He has shown Himself to be a great listener and comforter. We are learning to go to Him with our specific financial concerns and to give Him all the praise when He meets our needs in miraculous ways. Our time of financial readjustment has truly increased my prayer life as I've become more intimately acquainted with *Jehovah-Jireh*, my provider. I have learned what a detail-oriented, personal God He is. This experience has deepened my faith—a benefit I did not expect.

As we've walked through this time of going to God for everything we need, I've learned to trust in Him more completely. Though I'll talk about this in more detail later, I want to share some things that happened just last summer that illustrate how God answers even what most would call silly, insignificant prayers. Know, though, that nothing we pray is silly and insignificant to God!

+ In past summers, we'd gone to a farm and picked buckets of blueberries. But it was not cheap to buy the blueberries—and I knew that we didn't need to spend the money. So I told the Lord about how I wanted blueberries. I didn't really ask Him for blueberries, per se, I just told my Daddy how I was longing for some blueberries for making pancakes, muffins, cakes, and other dishes. Just a few days later, I was talking with a woman I barely knew, and she mentioned that she and her family would be going out of town for a few weeks. She said that she worried about their large blueberry bushes with no one to pick them—and would we like to come and help ourselves while they were gone? Would we! We were able to pick bags of blueberries—for free!

✦ My son needed a new bike to ride up to our neighborhood pool because his had been stolen. We simply did not have it in the budget to buy the new bike—and yet the mother's heart in me broke every time I saw him walking up to the pool while all the other kids rode past him. I told God how much it hurt and asked Him to provide my son with a bike when I could not. Just a few days later I was at a children's consignment store and there, for a very inexpensive price, was a bike that looked almost new and was the perfect size for my very tall son. Why was this bike at a children's consignment store that day? Because God orchestrated it so that I would find it. At least that's what I believe, and that's why I praised Him that day for answering this mother's prayer and taking care of yet another detail in my life.

✦ One day I was craving a good, old southern tomato sandwich, a staple of my summer diet. But we had no tomatoes. I was just about to get in the car and drive to a produce stand to buy the tomatoes when I felt God tell me not to go, but to wait for the tomatoes. What a strange response, I thought. But I obeyed, wondering what God was up to. Within the hour, my son ran in from the neighbor's house with several large, juicy ripe tomatoes in his hands. "Mom," he cried, "Miss Joyce had too many tomatoes and I told her you'd love to have some!" I didn't miss that opportunity to let my son know how God had used him to answer his mom's prayer.

✦ A new necklace was all the rage and caught my eye several times as I saw it on the necks of other women. Usually I'm not much of a jewelry person, but there was something different about this particular necklace. I even found one for a reasonable price at a little home jewelry show and had it in my hand to buy it when I felt God nudging me to put it back. "But it's a great price," I told God—as if He didn't know that. Again, I felt Him telling me to put it back. *I will provide*, I heard Him say. The following month we were visiting my stepsister, Becky, in Florida and I noticed that she was wearing that same necklace. I told her how much I liked it. "Oh," she replied. "Do you want one? Because I got one for a gift and certainly don't need two!" And just like that, I was the proud owner of a necklace I really wanted. And I didn't have to spend a dime.

These are just a few examples of the countless times that God has shown us that He hears our prayers, He cares about the details, and He will move on our behalf. Sometimes we just have to be patient. And sometimes we have to learn to take *no* for an answer. Because I've seen God provide in miraculous ways, I've learned that when He says no, there has to be a good reason. And I must accept His *no* and move on instead of brooding over it. This process has taught me much about holding the things of this earth lightly—and has drawn me closer to the Father's heart in the process. Through it all, we've indeed found hope in what could have been seen as a hopeless situation.

Do you need to find hope for your finances? The God of hope (Rom. 15:13) is waiting to show you the way out of debt and into freedom.

■ STUDY

Read Genesis 6:5; Luke 2:19; and Hebrews 4:12. How do these verses relate our thought lives to the condition of our hearts?

■ REFLECT, DISCUSS, PLAN

1. Was it a different concept for you to think of money as being tied to your heart attitude instead of your thought life?
2. What heart attitude do you struggle with the most—commitment, obedience, surrender, or prayer? Is there a part of you that

     still wants to control the situation and is hesitant about involving your heart in the process?

3. In the car that night prior to Christmas, we took a big step toward getting out of debt, as we verbally committed to each other to do whatever it took to get out of debt. Has there been a time when you've taken this step with your spouse? Does there need to be?

4. Have money problems been the lowest point in your marriage? If so, why do you think that is?

■ TAKE ACTION

Are you facing a particular situation that feels hopeless? (A bill that's due, large amounts of debt to pay off, a purchase that needs to be made but no money to make it, etc.) Write down Romans 15:13 and then spend time praying that verse aloud. If you're working through this book with your spouse, pray together.

Chapter 2

HITTING ROCK BOTTOM

Curt

The silence was growing uncomfortable.

The year was 1997. I was sitting in a chair across from a financial counselor who worked with a national charitable organization. The manila folder that held all of my family's financial information was open and spread out over her desk. I was there because one of Marybeth's friends was aware of my family's serious financial problems and had told her that this organization would be able to help. I walked into the office feeling hopeful, but the longer I sat, the more exposed and vulnerable I felt. I remember tightly gripping the arms of the old chair, forcing myself to stay seated, resisting the urge to spring out of the chair, grab all of my papers, and hurry away from the shame and humiliation that was engulfing me.

Still silent, the counselor's face reflected her confusion as she flipped through the budget sheets, bills, and past-due notices. I looked on her desk and let my eyes scan the names of the companies I owed money to. I thought about the magnitude of my problem and had to fight against the panic that was rising inside me. It seemed impossible to be able to clean up the financial mess I'd made. My stomach churned and my throat tightened. My mind went back in time, trying to mentally undo all the mistakes and unwise choices I'd made. I wished that I could grab hold of the "me" from years past and shake him, warning him of the problems he was creating for himself, problems from which no one would rescue him.

I sat in that chair feeling defeated and hopeless.

There'd been a time when I was filled with self-confidence. Marybeth and I were both rising seniors at North Carolina State University, earning good degrees. We'd mapped out our future and were sure that by following our plan we'd achieve success. I was getting an electrical engineering degree and dreamed of a job with a large salary. Marybeth and I had painted a picture of a life that included a typical upscale suburban family with 2.4 kids, a two-story brick house in the "right" neighborhood, perfectly manicured yard, sporty new cars, and country club membership.

My identity as a husband and father was wrapped up in making that dream a reality. Like most of my peers, I wanted it sooner rather then later. I didn't want to wait on anyone's timing other than my own, even if it meant having to live on credit to achieve my goals. I had no appreciation for the satisfaction of earning something over a long period of time. I falsely assumed that if the bank said I could afford it, then I could afford it. If I could make the monthly payment, then all was well.

In the five years between graduating from college and sitting in the counselor's chair, I'd learned that life has a funny way of messing up your best laid plans. We intended on spending a few years building a solid financial foundation with two incomes, but Marybeth had unexpectedly become pregnant soon after we were married, and we'd decided she should stay home with our son. Our income was limited to just my salary, and instead of creating and sticking to a budget that kept us from going into debt, we used credit cards to maintain a lifestyle well above our means.

We also made stupid decisions like buying new cars and later even trading them in for newer models. We bought our first home before we were ready. We had no savings, so we weren't prepared for those unexpected things that happen and require money to fix. After only five years of marriage, we owed thousands of dollars to the IRS, had two large student loans, were upside down in a car loan, had a house payment we could barely pay, and multiple credit cards with thousands of dollars owed on each. I was constantly juggling to keep everyone current, and failing more than succeeding. I became an expert at robbing Peter to pay Paul.

And then in the summer of 1996, the bottom dropped out. Our third child was born with a rare birth defect that required immediate and prolonged medical attention. Before I could truly understand the extent of his medical condition, we were incurring thousands of dollars of medical debt. Even with good insurance, we found ourselves getting past-due notices from doctors offices, hospitals, and specialists.

After years of treading water and barely staying afloat, our total debt was more then we could juggle. We were going under. I couldn't make all of our monthly payments without running out of money. After writing out all of our bills, I had nothing left for food, utilities, or gas. Creditors were calling our home nightly, demanding their payments. Our mailbox was flooded with late notices. Life was a daily panic attack, and our marriage was barely breathing. Marybeth and I had both grown to resent and blame each other for the mess our family had become. One day while driving to work, I saw a billboard advertising this financial counseling agency we'd heard about. In desperation, I called and made an appointment.

As the counselor shifted in her chair and looked up, my thoughts came back to the present. She began to talk, explaining the problems she saw in our family budget. Things I was already aware of. She went through the past-due bills, explaining what each company would probably do to collect what they were owed. Quite honestly, I don't remember many other specifics of what she said that day. All I remember was her final comment, a sentence that stuck with me and haunted me for months.

"I'm not really sure how I can help you. The only thing I can recommend is to declare bankruptcy."

My memories of the rest of that day are a blur. I didn't go back to my office, but aimlessly drove around Charlotte trying to fight off the feeling of overwhelming despair. My financial problems were affecting every area of my life. My marriage had suffered for years under the strain of trying to keep financially afloat. Marybeth and I had even been talking about divorce. I couldn't be the father that my kids deserved. I was constantly worried about our money problems and was angry and bad tempered all the time at home. I couldn't concentrate at work. I'm a salesman, and it's hard to sell something when your self-confidence has been eroded to nothingness. The Bible says that people in debt are slaves to their creditors (Prov. 22:7), and over time I'd come to believe that I had little self-worth. I thought about all these things as I drove around town.

I ended up that day at the bankruptcy courthouse. No words can describe the shame that covered me as I walked up those steps. I went there to stand in the lobby and imagine what it would be like to stand in front of a bankruptcy judge. I wanted to imagine the conflicting emotions of hearing that my debts were cleared but that my life was scarred with a bankruptcy judgment. I stood there in the lobby and tried to imagine what I would tell my wife and kids. I tried to imagine how I would explain this to my father. I let my mind explore my fears of failure and the fears that came from questions like "What would happen to our house?" and "How would we ever recover?" I stood there and watched the people come and go and imagined I was one of those leaving the courthouse to a new life free from debt but with the memory of innocence lost.

Something unexpected happened to me that afternoon in the courthouse as I stood and watched the people swirling around me. Something deep inside my soul awakened and spoke. My feelings of hopelessness and despair began to transform into anger and resolve. I got angry at myself for not listening to people from my past who'd tried to teach me about finances and budgeting. I got angry at the credit card companies who specifically targeted a college student and tempted him with easy money. To be honest, at the time, I even got angry at God for allowing all of these things to happen to me, including the problems with my son. Most importantly, I was frustrated for the stupid decisions I'd made and for not seeking out help earlier in my life. I walked out the courthouse doors and back to my car, determined to find a way to clean up the mess I'd made with money.

I've learned a lot about bankruptcy since then. I've learned that things like student loans and IRS debt don't get cleared. I've met many people who've filed for bankruptcy in the past but now regret the decision. Most filed out of fear, and really didn't understand the long-term implications of how it would affect their lives. Most now realize that, if in the same situation today, they'd be able to prepare a plan. They could clear their consumer debts over a two- or three-year period and not suffer the lingering credit and emotional effects that bankruptcy can bring.

A story in 2 Kings 4 relates how God helped a poor widow who came to the prophet Elisha begging for help. Her husband, a good man who served the Lord faithfully, died and left her with many debts. Creditors were coming to take her sons as slaves. Elisha told her what God wanted her to do to fix the problem, and the widow faithfully obeyed his instructions. God took the little bit of oil the woman owned and multiplied it by her big faith. God literally poured out His blessing on her. The widow was able to sell the oil God provided, pay off all her debts, and live on what was left over.

Three things from this passage stand out. First, the widow didn't keep her problems to herself. Her situation was desperate. Her sons were about to be taken away forever. Instead of hiding behind her shame, she humbled herself and asked someone for help. For years, I hid our family's financial problems from others. I kept telling myself that I'd get a handle on things and be able to turn our situation around. The opposite happened, and Marybeth and I slid deeper and deeper into debt. Only when I reached out to others and admitted that I didn't have all the answers did I start learning what I needed to know and seeing real improvements.

Second, the passage also demonstrates the widow's unquestioning faith. Elisha asked her to do something that didn't make sense. She only had a tiny bit of oil, but Elisha told her to get all the jars she could collect. Don't you think this sounded really strange to her? Can you imagine the response from her neighbors? Can you imagine the stares and comments she got as she went from house to house to collect the jars? But the widow ignored the opinions of others, stuck it out, and was obedient to what God asked her to do. Marybeth and I have found that getting out of debt requires a commitment and strategy that many of our friends and neighbors didn't understand. Many times in our journey, the reaction from others was harder to live with than the actual step we were taking to fix our problems.

The last thing that stands out is that God gave the widow just enough. She was able to collect the exact number of jars she needed to get just enough oil to pay off her debts. She even had just enough left over to live on. Even during the hardest part of our financial journey, Marybeth and I have always had just enough. We've had just enough to feed and clothe our kids. We've had just enough to pay cash to fix things that had broken. Unexpected things would happen to help us. Unexpected money would show up during lean times. People would help in unexpected ways. God was always present, always helping, always bringing us just enough.

Marybeth and I began our process of collecting jars, a process that wasn't simple or instantaneous. I realized that my pride had created many problems that needed to be addressed. I began reaching out to men in my church whom I could trust and asking for help. I started going to a Thursday morning men's meeting and opened up to the guys there about my struggles. An older gentleman in our church took me under his wing and not only paid a few of our smaller medical bills, but also introduced me to books by Larry Burkett, then president of Christian Financial Concepts. The men's group began reading *Business by the Book*, and I realized for the first time how much financial wisdom is in the Bible. To this day, I believe that because I humbled myself to other Christian men, God surrounded me with guys who could help me learn solid biblical principles for handling money. Years later, I still run into these men and am reminded of the power of the bond of Christian fellowship and how we, as brothers and sisters in

Christ, can help those around us simply by encouraging and supporting them.

Very slowly, things improved for Marybeth and me. Very slowly, God filled our jars and continued to provide just enough to help us begin fixing our financial mess. We also began to learn more of what God's Word says about finances. I went through the Crown Ministry counseling course, and discovered a hope in God's Word that had been missing years before in the counseling office I'd visited. Then, about four years ago as I was traveling out of state on a sales call and scanning the talk radio dial, I came upon a station that was carrying a broadcast from a guy named Dave Ramsey. I listened in fascination as he took phone call after phone call from people just like me. Person after person called in with problems that sounded impossible to solve, but he'd slowly take them through what he called his "baby steps" and "debt snowball." Each caller hung up with not only a solid plan, but a feeling of hope that had been absent only minutes before.

At this time Marybeth and I put ourselves on a debt elimination plan (more about that later) and did our best to follow it religiously. Over these past four years, we've learned many things about marriage and money that we'll share with you in this book. We'll tell you about our mistakes as well as our successes. We've learned how difficult it can be to swim against the tide of our culture, which overwhelms us with offers of easy credit and tells us that spending more is the key to happiness and security. Most importantly, we'll share how we found that God can use the subject of money to transform our lives and our marriage.

We're learning to trust God when things seem hopeless. We've found biblical principles regarding money that God gives us to guide and teach us. We're finding that our Father in heaven loves us more than we ever understood and fights alongside us during difficult times. He wants us to bring our problems to Him and to trust and have faith in His immeasurable love for us. Like the widow in 2 Kings, God had been slowly filling our jars with just enough. Applying the financial principles we've found in Scripture has helped us pay off our debts and is guiding us toward true financial freedom.

There's a short verse in the fifth chapter of Mark that I carry with me every day. Jesus is approached by a father whose daughter is deathly ill. The father wants Jesus to come to his home to heal his little girl. The man is filled with grief, falls at Jesus' feet, and pleads "fervently" with Jesus to come to his home.

Most of us have faced desperate financial situations. Confronted with what seems to be impossible, we've been paralyzed by fear and fallen at the feet of Jesus pleading with Him to come help us make things better. Ten years ago, I was sitting in a financial counselor's office, silently begging God to help my family. This New Testament father was no different. Faced with a hopeless situation, a father came to Christ for help. But as they were walking back to his home, the father hears the worst. A servant approaches to tell him that his daughter has died.

The foreclosure notice comes in the mail. The car is repossessed. Our wages are garnished. The boss comes into our office and quietly shuts the door. We put all of our efforts into fixing situations only to find them spiraling out of control. But in our darkest moments, hope can break through. Jesus grabs this heartbroken father's shoulders, looks him in the eyes, and whispers into the deepest part of his soul.

"Don't be afraid; just believe" (Mark 5:36b).

As Marybeth and I have struggled to overcome our financial difficulties, I've gone to that verse a lot. "Don't be afraid; just believe." When my wife and I weren't getting along and were fighting over bills, "Don't be afraid; just believe." When my office's sales dipped and my income took a hit, "Don't be afraid; just believe." When the bills stacked up, things were breaking down, and I struggled with staying current, "Don't be afraid; just believe." When the economic forecast is grim and the cost of everything seems to be rising, "Don't be afraid; just believe." When everything seems to be going wrong and I feel alone . . .

"Don't be afraid; just believe."

It's not easy for me to follow that instruction. My mind goes in a thousand directions and I worry about many things. I want to wrap my arms around my wife and children and protect them from harm. I want to stand between my family and all the things that can come and hurt them including financial problems. Somewhere along the way as I sank deeply into debt, I lost the innocence and eternal optimism of youth. I've watched good people, good men, good families go through financial devastation. And at times I, too, get scared.

Over the past four years, as Marybeth and I worked our way out of financial bondage, Christ's words of hope continued to burn in my mind and give me hope. Time and time again, I grab hold of these words and keep them close to my heart. Over and over again, I hear Him say these words of comfort and protection. As Marybeth and I share the story of our financial struggles, our prayer is that you'll begin to place your hope in an eternal truth. Regardless of where you are on this financial journey, whether you're completely out of debt or facing bankruptcy, God's love for you is deeper then the deepest ocean. You are His child and He loves you with the full passion of His heart. You can walk in the confidence that Christ's words were spoken for you.

"Don't be afraid; just believe."

■ STUDY

Read the following verses, which were referenced in this chapter: 2 Kings 4:1–7; Proverbs 22:7; and Mark 5:35–42.

■ REFLECT, DISCUSS, PLAN

1. How do you feel about your current financial situation? Are you scared? Encouraged? Hopeful?
2. If you're currently in debt, the Bible says that you're a slave to that creditor. Would you agree or disagree with that statement? If you were to answer this question honestly, how has carrying a large amount of debt affected the feelings you have for yourself?
3. If you have consumer debt, how committed are you to paying it off? Have you developed a plan, and will you and your spouse hold each other accountable to it? If you don't have consumer

debt, how committed are you to staying debt free? Discuss practical ways that you could be held accountable either to following your plan for paying off your debts or your plan for staying out of debt.

■ TAKE ACTION

Find a time when you and your spouse can have an honest discussion about how you're feeling about your finances. List out all your debts, smallest to largest, and talk about your commitment to paying them off. How quickly could you begin? How long would it take you to become free of all your debts?

Commit to supporting each other regardless of how desperate your situation feels. Pray that God will not only restore your hope, but help you develop a plan to achieve and maintain financial freedom.

Chapter 3

UNLOADING
FINANCIAL BAGGAGE

Marybeth

We'd been married only a few months and I was already finding out that marriage was not the cakewalk I'd hoped for. One of the first issues to pop up between us was our different approach to finances. Only three months into the marriage, as my friend and I were driving to the tiny apartment I shared with my new husband, a red and white Bronco came flying up behind us. The driver of the Bronco was flagging us down and weaving in and out of traffic, trying to catch us. I looked back at this unfamiliar vehicle, trying to get a good look at the driver's face. I couldn't imagine who'd be trying to talk to us, as I knew no one who drove a red and white Bronco. Finally my friend Karen got a good look at the driver as he worked his way through the traffic. "Isn't that Curt?" she asked.

"No!" I replied a little too defensively as I craned my neck to get a good look. I noticed the driver waving at me and reluctantly admitted that it did, indeed, look like my husband—who had never looked more like a stranger to me. What was he doing in a red Bronco? He drove a little red Toyota. Which was paid for. As Karen drove me on to our apartment, Curt followed closely behind. I was filled with questions for him and my anger mounted as we drove.

When we got to our apartment, Karen hastily made her exit, giving us some much-needed privacy. Curt was grinning from ear to ear as he pointed to his new toy. "Do you like it?" he asked.

"Please tell me you didn't buy that!" I responded angrily.

"Well, no," he said. "I mean, I haven't filled out any paperwork yet. I wanted to show it to you first."

"Good. Then just take it back where you got it and stay away from car dealerships from now on. We can't afford to be buying cars when you have a perfectly good, paid-for car that runs just fine."

He wasn't going for it. "But this car is cool, and it's our school colors. I don't really like my car anymore. I'm tired of it."

"Well you should have thought of that before you got married. You can have a new car or you can have a wife. Seems to me you already made that choice."

We stared at each other. Although we both knew I was right about our financial situation, he wasn't ready to give up his new toy. Eventually he did take the Bronco back, but not without letting me know how disappointed he was in me for not playing along with his little fantasy. After he left I sat alone in our apartment wondering how in the world this marriage was going to work when two people had such different viewpoints.

This was our married life for many years. Our marriage was, in fact, a financial disaster waiting to happen. Neither of us came into marriage financially prepared. We didn't know the first thing about budgeting our money, saving, or planning ahead. We lived life day by day with little regard for what might come. We were still in college, with both of us taking on hefty loans just to get by. When I got pregnant just three months into the marriage, I was forced to reduce my work hours and take on more college credit hours just to finish by the time the baby was born.

Our debts multiplied at amazing rates as we did stupid things like finance a video camera because we "needed" one to film our unborn child. We took out every college loan available to us and, after trying to juggle college, work, and time together, reduced our work hours.

Additionally there were the expenses of a new baby to consider. The stress of our situation affected the way we treated each other. The more we spent, the angrier I became. The more I launched into one of my tirades, the further from me Curt withdrew. I looked to him to save us and he cringed when he saw me coming.

The reality is, we both needed help where finances were concerned. My way of coping with our financial problems was to take out more loans. Far from being worried about how we'd pay for all the debt we were racking up, I took much comfort in knowing there was money in the bank. I'm the child of a single mom and finances were often a concern in our home, so I was constantly worried about running out of money. Curt was prone to make purchases based on how he'd look to other people, partly because he struggled with a need to impress people with what he had. Neither of us had the foggiest notion of how to communicate effectively about money. And we certainly hadn't a clue about how to execute a plan for our finances.

To us, money wasn't an element of our marriage to be planned for and enjoyed; rather, money problems were something to be endured and addressed only when absolutely necessary. At times those money problems caught up to us with a vengeance. Times like these taught us just how much our lack of preparation in managing money could affect us.

Curt

One of the hardest decisions I ever made early on in our marriage was to take a job washing cars. Marybeth and I had graduated from North Carolina State University in May of 1992, and our first child was due in mid-August. I was getting desperate to find a "real" job using my college degree. The debts we incurred during our last year of school were coming due, and our first child was about to be born. At that time, our country was in the midst of a recession, and I couldn't find anyone interested in a newly graduated electrical engineer who wanted to be in technical sales. Although Marybeth and I were living with my dad, I felt an internal desperation to start earning an income. So when I drove by a local car wash where I'd worked many summers during college and noticed they were hiring, I pulled in and applied.

After a few weeks at the car wash, I was fortunate enough to find a job with a textile manufacturing company, and for the first time had a nice salary with good benefits. Things were looking up! Then, six months later, I was able to get a sales job with a major air conditioner manufacturing company. It was a great opportunity with a large earning potential. However, I was considered a contract employee, which affected how my taxes were handled. The company human resources person explained to me that I was considered self-employed and had to manage my quarterly tax payments and business expenses. They recommended that I hire and work with an accountant who'd make sure that I kept up with my tax liability.

I chose to ignore that advice and handle everything myself. It wouldn't be the first—or last—time that my ego and pride caused me problems. After a year of training with this company, I started operating as a 100 percent commissioned, self-employed salesman. I started making good money, but instead of putting a portion aside for taxes every month, I used every dime I was making, trying to keep up with all of our other bills. Marybeth and I had no spending plan, and we didn't talk about any of the decisions I was making month to month. I justified keeping our problems hidden by telling myself that I was protecting her from the stress of everything that was going wrong.

A problem can remain hidden in a marriage for only so long. One afternoon a few years after starting this sales position, Marybeth went out to get the mail. In it was a letter from the IRS. She read their notice of taxes past due and immediately called me. Not only had I not been paying my quarterly taxes, but when I filed our taxes that year, I didn't have the money to pay the government the $10,000 we owed. The letter they sent to inform us of our problem was threatening, and the fights Marybeth and I had afterward were almost the final nail in the coffin of our fragile marriage. I'd hidden things from her and abused the trust she had placed in me. Instead of working as a team to manage our household finances and developing a solid plan, we were living in the middle of a financial mess. We fought and argued every time we tried to talk about money. The stress of all our debt, which now included owing the IRS, seemed more than this young marriage could stand.

Marybeth

Another challenge in Curt's and my marriage was understanding our love languages. *The Five Love Languages*, by Gary Chapman, helped me understand my spouse on many levels—finances included.[1] This book outlines five ways that we receive love—physical touch and closeness, words of affirmation, acts of service, gift giving, or quality time. How we express love is closely tied to how we receive love. I came to see that the way we each interpreted the love our partner was attempting to show was a large part of our failure to connect where money is concerned.

I was raised by a mom who expressed her love through gift giving. Since my love language is quality time, my mom and I often combined the two by spending a day shopping with a stop for lunch along the way. Because I have such fond memories of these times spent with my mom, quality time and gift giving got linked in my mind. I came to believe that love meant spending money. Thus, the best way for Curt to show me he loved me was to take me to the mall and buy me something— spending lots of quality time with me in the process. This filled my love tank, but also got us deeper into debt. The trouble was, if he suggested not spending money I interpreted it as him not loving me.

Curt, on the other hand, thrives on words of affirmation. He, like many men, craves my respect and my encouragement as he attempts to do a good job as a husband and provider. During those troubled times, he longed to hear me say that he was man enough in my eyes, but he mostly heard that he was failing me in a thousand little ways. As I ranted and raved over his spending habits and stressed about our mounting debt and lack of money, he heard, "You aren't good enough." Though I had no idea at the time, my words were eroding the very foundation of our marriage. We were both left feeling alone and disconnected as our needs for love went unmet and our expectations for each other came up short. We simply didn't know how to speak each other's love language.

Through sheer tenacity, we hung in there. Not because we possessed any special staying power but because we simply refused to give up on this marriage. Some of our determination, I will admit now, was just to prove the naysayers wrong. We'd show them we could make it against all odds. And with all the baggage—financial and otherwise—we were carrying, the odds were certainly against us.

Learning to speak the other person's love language was a step in the right direction. Not only did we learn to speak words of love, we learned to recognize and appreciate each other's efforts. This was a huge breakthrough, both financially and emotionally.

What Money Isn't

We learned a lot during that time about what money is and what it is not.[2] Through financial classes at our church and reading books on the subject, we realized how much we had to learn and how far we had to go to get our money situation under control. It wouldn't happen overnight or through a quick fix. Most of all, we saw that at the root of our issues was a very real need for growth in our relationship with God. The more we learned of Him, the more we recognized our need to adjust our views on money, the more we desired to forgive each other and show each other the grace we both needed. Slowly, lovingly, God taught us what He had to say about material possessions, contentment, and giving. The more we learned, the more we realized what money is not.

Not a Measure of Love

I used to think that my husband's love could be measured in dollars and cents. I thought that he needed to prove his love for me by buying presents for me and making me feel secure. The trouble is, I realized that the momentary happiness I felt when he did buy little tokens certainly didn't last. I found that material gifts did not equal love, and that a deep, abiding love could not be purchased. I had to experience the staying power of a love that is proven over time and through tests. As I embraced this new perspective, I realized how silly it was to measure the depth of Curt's love by his willingness to spend money on shiny baubles, expensive dinners, and flowers that would certainly die before the credit card bill arrived. These days I'm what I like to call a "cheap date." Dinner at a fast-food restaurant suits me just fine, as long as we have a few moments to connect and finish a sentence. And flowers? He knows that a sweet tea at Chick-fil-A speaks volumes of love to me and only costs $2!

Not a Gauge of Worth

For a long time, we both relied on external factors—the house we lived in, the car we drove, the clothes we wore, and what we had—to give us a sense of being valued. God had to show us through His Word that our financial picture had no bearing on our value in His eyes. He does not judge our bank account, but our hearts. As we began to make Him the priority of our lives, we cared less about the external factors and more about the climate of our hearts. We learned that God cares most that we are in relationship with Him, and it is through that relationship that we must derive our sense of being valued—not by the world, but by the God of the universe.

Not a Reward for Spiritual Living

I think we both believed that if we were good enough Christians, God would reward us with financial gain. As we struggled with money and debt, we wondered why God was abandoning us. We questioned His love for us and doubted His promises. We had to learn that God's economy is the opposite of ours. Matthew 20:16 tells us that "the last will be first, and the first will be last." We began to recognize God's blessings when they came along. In God's economy, blessings come in the form of humility, purity of heart, grace, love, and peace. These are rewards that the world fails to see, and yet they are priceless.

Not a Guarantee of Satisfaction

Money does not bring happiness. Just look at wealthy people and celebrities. Many of them are the most miserable people you'll ever meet. Recent headlines about the misadventures of several rich young celebrities have brought this home to me more than ever. By the world's standards, they have it all, yet they're still searching and obviously lacking. As God's creations, we long to connect with our Creator. We crave fellowship with Him and relationship with Him. Money is a pitiful substitute. Our souls cry out for something greater—something deeper, richer, and much more permanent than what the world's economy has to offer. We followed the world's lead and began our marriage looking to money for that satisfaction. And we came up empty every time.

What Money Is

As God showed us what money is not, He simultaneously replaced those views with what He intended money to be. We now see what money is.

A Temptation

Money is a temptation to be self-reliant. When we allow money to meet our needs and desires and to be the answer to all our problems, we eliminate our need for a heavenly Father. Yet what God desires is total dependence on Him. Satan knows when money is your weak link, and he will use it to defeat you if he can. We had to learn that there are weak areas in our finances—old habits that are easy to slip back into—that we must guard against. We can't fall victim to temptation as we know that with just a few bad decisions we can lose the ground we've gained.

A Teacher

Money, as we've said, affects every part of our lives. Money even affects our health—especially when faced with the chronic stress of debt. When we're facing money problems, studies show that, "The body reacts with a 'fight-or-flight' response, releasing adrenaline and the stress hormone cortisol. That helps you react fast in an emergency, but if the body stays in this high gear too long, those chemicals can wreak physical havoc in numerous systems—everything from a rise in blood pressure and heart rate to problems with memory, mood, digestion, even the immune system."[3]

When even your health is affected, you realize just how powerful a factor your finances can be. Something that can make this much impact in our lives is sure to become a valuable teacher as well. For the sake of our physical and spiritual well-being, Curt and I have learned how to manage our money, learning valuable lessons about trust, resourcefulness, patience, and responsibility in the process.

A Tool

With each lesson, we've walked away a little wiser and a little better equipped for the next time. We're learning to be better stewards and to give freely. A friend recently reminded me that when we hold on to what we have with a clenched fist, God can't put anything into that hand. Yet when we open our hands to give, then our hands are open to His blessings. I love this word picture and what it means for us when we willingly and lovingly open our hands to give to others. Curt and I have been wonderfully blessed as a result of giving, in addition to being a tool to bless others.

A Testimony

Our struggle with finances is a huge part of our marriage testimony. Money plays into so much of our married lives. We've felt hopelessness and despair, wondering if we'd ever get out of our money pit. In Curt's financial counseling to numerous couples, and through my writing, we've been given a ministry that testifies of God's goodness. We can offer hope to couples who find themselves in similar situations. We can turn back, as Jesus told Peter to do. In Luke 22:32 He said, "But I have prayed for you, Simon, that your faith may not fail. And when you have turned back, strengthen your brothers." As we look back, we see two very confused and ignorant young people God placed on a path to financial wisdom of *His* design. Our goal is to point others toward that same path.

God has used these lessons to mold and shape our character. These lessons have, in fact, been woven into the very fabric of our marriage. Though none of them were learned overnight, over time we filed them away one by one. Some of them took longer to seep in than others. All of these lessons became a part of who we are as individuals and as a couple. They have ignited in us a passion to share what God has done for us, and what He can do for you if you give Him room to work in your heart and in your life.

■ STUDY

Read 1 Samuel 16:7; Psalm 127:2; Ecclesiastes 5:10; and Luke 12:15. How do these verses pertain to the lessons we learned and shared with you?

■ REFLECT, DISCUSS, PLAN

1. Name a time in your marriage when your different approaches to finances became glaringly obvious. If it's not too painful, reminisce about this with your spouse.
2. In the "what money isn't" list, which one do you struggle with the most?
3. In the "what money is" list, name one in which you've experienced a recent victory.

■ TAKE ACTION

Spend some time in prayer—either alone or with your spouse if you feel comfortable—asking God to help you see money by His design and not by the world's. As you encounter situations this week, determine whether you are seeing money as it is or as it isn't. Ask God to help you recognize wrong thinking about money and replace those thoughts with a proper perspective.

Chapter 4

BECOMING A TEAM

Marybeth

Curt's first job right out of college was not his dream job by any stretch. He took it just to put a roof over our heads and pay the bills. But, as we've said, the pay was not really enough to make ends meet, and we struggled from month to month. Every month it seemed we had the same conversation: Should I go to work and provide a second income? So when he had the chance to get a job he really liked and that would pay much better, we jumped at the chance. Never mind that this job involved us moving halfway across the country for six months while he went to a training class.

We gutted it out for those six months and returned to our hometown. I got us settled in a little house we bought and Curt got down to business. He worked hard as a junior salesman teamed with an older salesman who challenged him a bit more than he liked. The relationship between them became tense and he began to wonder how long he could stay in that job.

The longer he worked for this company, however, the more money he made. As he developed skills and relationships, his sales numbers went up. With higher sales, we received higher commissions. I was thrilled, finally able to buy what we needed without fretting about it. I remember one Christmas in particular, I went to the mall, searching for a red tablecloth for our holiday meal. I chose one that was bright red, embellished with holly leaves. It was exactly what I wanted, and I bought it on the spot. I was able to pay for it with cash, and I didn't have to wonder if there was money in the bank to cover it. I felt proud as I placed my purchase in the stroller basket and wheeled my two children out of the mall. I felt like Mary Tyler Moore singing "You're gonna make it after all." I all but threw my hat in the air!

To this day that shopping trip stands out in my memory. I distinctly remember thinking, *We're out of the woods now. We'll never have to worry about money again.* I felt secure and safe. Our grown-up life was beginning and the future seemed bright and full of promise. Little did I know that in just six months Curt would change jobs, and our lives would be drastically altered.

Although to me life seemed good, to Curt life was quickly becoming a nightmare as his relationship with his senior partner steadily declined. Desperate to get out of a bad situation, he jumped at the chance to take another job with a different company. The job didn't conflict with his noncompete clause and was with a company he liked, working with people he admired. Just what he was looking for. There was only one catch—this job paid less than what he'd been making. Overnight, our income was cut in half. My newfound financial security, it seemed, had been blown apart.

In the previous chapter, we talked about the financial baggage each spouse carries into the marriage. For me, this financial baggage included a history of growing up in a single-parent household where money was always scarce. I always felt the strain of not having enough money—not being able to buy the "cool" clothes I wanted as a young teen, eating cheap meals, never being able to go out to dinner. Each year I was told that Christmas would be slim—again. While none of this was devastating by any means, I did often wish that we had more money. I felt anxious about our financial situation and knew my mother worried over our needs being met. As a child, I made a vow that I would not live that way. I promised myself that once I could make decisions, I would not have financial problems. Ah, the ignorance of youth.

When Curt changed jobs, then, and our income was reduced, his decision stirred up those long-ago feelings of not being financially secure. Once again I was in a position of not having enough money and feeling stretched thin. My little-girl vows did not hold up in the wake of my husband's choices. Ultimately, I felt betrayed and abandoned by him. This was a tough time in our marriage—not just financially, but in the way we related to each other. I began to lash out at him and blame him for our situation. I didn't feel that he had upheld his vow to take care of me or our children. In short, I was angry. When I tried to tell him how I felt, he would throw his hands up in exasperation and say, "Well, what do you want me to do about it now?"

The next several years consisted of job changes and searching. One year, Curt held three different jobs. He ended up doing the exact job he'd left a year earlier when working for a competitor. His income had improved slightly, but nowhere near what he once earned. Our marriage showed the effects of the financial and emotional stress of this time. To be honest, I didn't think I'd ever get over my anger toward him for "what he had done to me." Yes, I know how selfish that was.

All of this took a toll on how we responded to each other. God has wired women in a certain way. We long to be cared for and protected by our husbands—including financially. And God has wired men in a certain way. They have a strong need to be affirmed by their wives, to be respected and seen as good providers. Paul refers to this innate wiring when he warns men to *love* their wives, and warns wives to *respect* their husbands (Eph. 5:33). Paul knew what each spouse would struggle with. He knew where each needed to be reminded of his or her weakness. This period in our marriage was definitely a time for our weak spots to show.

Based on our experience, we've learned five basic areas where couples encounter problems in the area of finances:

1. *Communication*: not learning to communicate about money effectively, which leads to fighting and blaming.

2. *Budget*: not learning to create a budget and communicate about the budget.
3. *Unexpected expenses*: not planning for those little surprises in life that happen to everyone and not creating a fund to cover them.
4. *Home purchases*: buying a home too soon because it's "the thing to do" or buying a home that eats up too much of the budget.
5. *Spending money before you have it/taking on debt*: not saving money for purchases and falling into the "buy now/pay later" trap.

We'd made mistakes and poor decisions in all of these areas. We had a lot of ground to cover if we were ever going to stop fighting about our financial problems and start fixing them. We needed to become a team. This involved learning to commit, communicate, and construct.

Commit

In becoming a team, even more important than being committed to each other was committing our finances to God. Doing so was a battle for us. Neither one of us wanted to surrender control of our money to God. We wanted to feel like we were in control, making our own decisions and handling things on our own. While we attended church and went through the motions of Christianity, our hearts were not invested in His will for us. Like spoiled children, we didn't want an authority in our lives telling us what we could and could not do. Because our loving heavenly Father cares enough to let us have free will, He let us languish in this state for those first several years of our marriage. We foolishly thought that we had all the wisdom we needed and could handle whatever came our way, financial or otherwise. Meanwhile our decisions and our circumstances were causing our finances and our marriage to become a bigger mess with every passing year.

Deuteronomy 8:17–18 says, "You may say to yourself, 'My power and the strength of my hands have produced this wealth for me.' But remember the LORD your God, for it is he who gives you the ability to produce wealth, and so confirms his covenant, which he swore to your forefathers, as it is today." We had deceived ourselves into thinking that we could make our own way. Even as we submitted more and more of our lives to God, control of our finances was something we held back. We held our cards close to the vest, not wanting to lay them out on the table. Not wanting to give God access.

Fear held us back. What if He wanted all of our money? What if He required us to give up nice things? What if He called us to a life of deprivation and poverty? Through prayer and time in His word, we finally reached the ends of ourselves. Like Jacob wrestling with God, we had our time on the mat. As we limped away, we were acutely aware of one thing: none of it mattered but Him. And in that moment, we found freedom. Only through humbly submitting every aspect of our lives to God were we able for the first time to feel a peace about our finances and a union in our marriage. Call it a miracle, call it super-natural, call it anything you want. But committing our finances to God was the first step to becoming a team.

Communicate

Money is hard to talk about. Issues of pride, inadequacy, resent-ment, and shame get wrapped up in the conversation, resulting in hurt feelings, isolation, and even lying to each other. In the early days of our marriage, I don't think we had a single conversation about money that didn't end in a fight. Hurt feelings overrode our ability to reach out to each other and it stayed that way for years. Eventually, through church classes, personal counseling, and some key books, we were able to take those first tentative steps toward each other.

When talking about money, it's important to remember one thing: your spouse is not your enemy. Sometimes it might feel like his bad decision or her spending habits have landed you where you are, but don't aim your frustration at the person who is your partner. Satan will wage a campaign to convince you to do exactly that. He will tell you that you deserve more respect, someone gentler, someone smarter in your corner. He will urge you that you need to stand up for your rights and make your opinion known no matter whose feelings get hurt. His name means, "One who comes between," and that's what he's good at— coming between two people. He knows if he can divide you, he can break down your marriage. When I start to feel frustrated about finances or when walking through a particularly difficult time, I remember this verse: "For our struggle is not against flesh and blood, but against the rulers, against the authorities, against the powers of this dark world and against the spiritual forces of evil in the heavenly realms" (Eph. 6:12). I have to identify my enemy—and my enemy is not my spouse. This is so important to remember as we work to communicate about money.

There are three important reasons to communicate:

1. *To help each other understand the real financial picture of your home.* This understanding is twofold, and includes calculating the actual dollars-and-cents of your finances, and identifying the spending patterns that got you where you are. By communicating calmly and talking things through, heated emotions and unrealistic expectations can be shelved, and objectives and plans can be made.
2. *To hold each other accountable in spending habits and patterns.* By talking things through, you can establish checks and balances to head off problems before they take root.
3. *To build trust.* As you learn to communicate without tears and accusations, you find that camaraderie springs up between you. You feel linked in a purposeful way—working through problems together and facing tough challenges as a unified front. As you accept each other's advice and experience victories, a new level of trust is created. Where once there was bitterness, now there is hope.

As Curt and I recognized the importance of communication, we had to find points of connection that would make our communication efforts healthy and purposeful. Here are some things that have worked for us, but I can't stress enough that these are just ideas. What works for one couple may not work for another.

1. *Designate a financial leader.* One person will most likely be the financial point person in the marriage. This person may be more organized or numbers oriented. Whether husband or wife, the point is, that person is the one who pays the bills, balances the checkbook, and keeps up with accounts. This doesn't mean that the other person is hereby absolved of any financial commitment. It just means that one person is more detail minded and better equipped to handle finances. It's important to note that usually the person who does not do the nitty-gritty management side of the finances still has much to offer. Typically, this person is more visionary in his or her approach and can help cast a vision and project ideas for the overall financial picture. Whether you are the visionary or the point person, you still have to listen to the other person and engage in what's going on with the finances.

2. *Have regular "state of the union" meetings.* In these meetings discuss the following:
   + The bills to be paid
   + Your spending for that pay period—including any items needed
   + Unexpected expenses that need to be addressed
   + Any budget adjustments that need to be made in certain categories
   + Whether your spending is on track for that paycheck
   + How your financial goals are looking
   + Worries or concerns for either spouse
   + Any large expenses coming up that need to be saved for
   + How to allot any extra money you're expecting (commission checks, tax returns, bonuses, side job income, etc.)

This time is best opened and closed in prayer. If praying together is awkward at first, pray individually before you sit down. Put this meeting time on the calendar and stick to it. We suggest you meet weekly at first. Over time and with good habits, this regular sit-down time can stretch to bimonthly or monthly.

3. *Consider a secondary account.* This is not to be confused with having separate accounts, which we strongly advise against. If busyness is hindering you from being able to connect often enough, think about opening up a second account for one person to use with a designated amount of money deposited in it each pay period. When we were first getting a handle on our finances, this was a solution for us. In the midst of learning to handle money and learning to talk regularly, we knew that some things were simply going to fall through the cracks. We knew that our best bet was to create an account for me to use and manage apart from our main account. Curt and I settled on an amount to be deposited each pay period based on an agreed budgeted amount. We used this method for years. I ran our household while he paid the bills and other large expenses. From this account, I was to pay for groceries, toiletries, medicines, doctor visits, and needs for our children. If I felt I needed more money, I discussed it with him. For us, this separate account was not a permanent solution, but it did teach both of us to manage our monthly expenses without getting into more debt. (This is similar to the "cash envelope system" other financial experts recommend, where the money required for budgeted items such as groceries and gas are withdrawn at the beginning of each pay period and kept in separate, labeled envelopes. Thus, if $500 is budgeted for food during a pay period, then that amount is withdrawn in cash, put in an envelope label "groceries," and used during that pay period as needed. The intent is to use that exact amount on groceries every month. The trick is not pulling from one envelope to cover overspending from another envelope. If you are comfortable with handling large amounts of cash, this option might be one to try.)

4. *Use e-mail as a means of communication.* As I mentioned earlier, plain old busyness can cause a communication disconnect. Especially if you're in the throes of raising kids and building careers. We've found e-mail to be a convenient link to each other during our busy days. I can send Curt an e-mail if he is traveling, listing my latest expenses so he can deduct them instead of waiting until he gets home. He e-mails me the latest budget categories and how much is remaining in each category. With these little touch points built into our routine, there's little room for miscommunication about what we're facing financially.

5. *Don't keep secrets.* If you're keeping secrets from your spouse, it's time to lay it all out on the table. Be honest. Don't hide money from each other or cover your spending by hiding purchases and lying. Confess your past mistakes to each other and agree to start fresh, with no lies in your financial future. Ask someone you trust to hold you accountable not to lie to your spouse. Pray regularly for the strength to break out of this pattern of behavior that, for some, is a way of life. One survey stated that "36% of men and 40% of women confess that they had at one time or another lied to their spouse about the price of something they bought."[1] This same article said that lying about money is the most common lie between spouses. While it might be common, it's not good for the marriage. A marriage built on lies is sure to crumble over time. The lies become cracks in the foundation, deteriorating trust and breaking down the potential for communication.

Finally, you can learn to be each other's cheerleader, spurring each other on through areas of struggle. Curt changed jobs several more times before he ended up in his current one. So we had a long journey back to a place of stability. The darkest time of all came when he worked with a company that was last in his industry. The company's market presence determined how much money he earned as a salesman. Getting beat by other companies caused our standard of living to be reduced, surviving on his minimal paycheck with no commissions. During those years our income hovered at poverty level. Every day he suited up and went out to fight a losing battle. His sales meetings, he told me, were nothing but a group of men talking about how defeated they were. I soon noticed that this attitude of defeat was seeping into every area of his life. He adopted the mantle of "loser," and it affected his outlook, his countenance, and ultimately our home. As he drifted farther and farther away from me, I was never more painfully aware of how much a man's job defines him.

I remember that as I climbed into the shower every day, I prayed for our situation and for Curt. God seemed to be silent, yet I was certain that I needed to keep believing in Curt and encouraging him. I was to lift him up—walking a delicate balance between being his cheerleader and just allowing him to vent sometimes. This was a time for me to communicate to him how much I supported and believed in him as the leader of our home and the provider of our family. There were times, I confess, that I didn't think he even heard me. But I kept talking, pouring into him the best way I knew how. Mostly I just wanted to build him up to become the man I believed God had created him to be and not the broken down, defeated, shell of a man he had morphed into over a period of years.

Curt

As Marybeth described, this was a very low period in our marriage and in my life. The Bible says that to be in debt is to live as a slave, and I felt the emotions of that biblical truth every morning when I faced my day. Not only were we struggling with the burden of being thousands and thousands of dollars in debt, but now my career seemed to be at a dead end. Every day I got up and went to work in an atmosphere where last place was accepted as normal. Over time, I quit believing in myself. I questioned my decisions, the value I brought to the marketplace, and my self-worth.

It was hard for Marybeth to know how to manage our relationship during this time. There were moments when I needed to vent, times I needed encouragement, and times I needed her to challenge me about the beliefs I held. Most importantly, she simply prayed for me with an unwavering belief in my potential. God gave her a vision of the man I could become. She used love and words of encouragement to reignite a passion in my soul to make the career change that was long overdue. Her continued support gave me the strength to come to her and say, "I'm not taking this anymore. I'm going to find a job where I'm valued."

Marybeth

I learned from this period of our lives that communication about finances takes many forms. Sometimes we have to communicate our unwavering belief in each other and sometimes the best communication is simply to pray, interceding on behalf of your spouse and your marriage.

Construct

Once you commit your finances to God and begin to communicate with each other, it's important to construct a plan for conquering your financial problems—together. A home isn't built without a blueprint, and your financial house can't be built without one, either. For some, this will be nothing more than reclaiming something you once knew but lost sight of. For others there will be a huge learning curve filled with peaks and valleys. We'll cover how to construct this plan in the next several chapters. By walking through the first three things you must do (chapter 5), creating a budget (chapter 6), and reducing your spending (chapter 7), you'll have the knowledge base necessary to construct a sturdy, reliable financial house—a place where your money, and your family, will be safe for years to come.

■ STUDY

Read Proverbs 14:1; 24:3–4; Matthew 12:25; and 1 Timothy 5:8.

■ REFLECT, DISCUSS, PLAN

1. Of the five areas where couples make financial mistakes or poor decisions—communication, budgeting, unexpected expenses, home purchase, taking on debt—which are you struggling with the most at this time?
2. Of the three areas of team building—commit, communicate, construct—which do you feel you and your spouse already have a handle on?
3. How are Proverbs 14:1 and 1 Timothy 5:8 related? Why do you think these verses are included with this chapter?

■ TAKE ACTION

Schedule your first "state of the union" meeting with your spouse. Get it on the calendar and prepare for it with prayer. If you already do this, schedule a time to plan and dream about your financial future. Make this a time of celebration over what God has done in your lives and what you anticipate Him doing in the future.

Chapter 5

MOVING MONEY MOUNTAIN

Marybeth

Almost six years ago, we took the plunge and decided it was time to paint our house. Curt had been promised a commission check that would cover the cost of painting the house, and we debated using that money to hire someone instead of doing the job ourselves. I was due any day with our fifth child, and both of us wondered how likely it would be that Curt would have time to paint the house himself. One Saturday morning, he decided to go outside and give it a try. Several hours later, he came in, frustrated. "It's just too big a job!" he announced. "It would take me a year of Saturdays to paint this house!" He asked me for the name of a painter I knew, and the very next week, we hired him to paint our house a lovely yellow with green shutters. It cost us $5,000.

The trouble was, Curt's commission check had not come in yet. Some paperwork problems as well as some changes at his work had delayed it. We made the decision to go ahead with the painting and put the $5,000 on a credit card, reasoning that we'd pay the card off when we got the commission check. There was only one hitch in our little plan—we never did get that commission check. Curt's company restructured and the commission check disappeared into a corporate black hole. We were left with a $5,000 debt we had no way to pay off. Not to mention a new baby and all those expenses.

Across the street from us, our neighbor Tommy slowly and methodically began painting his house himself. He did a little at a time, putting in time on Saturdays between his construction job and coaching Little League. It took him about a year, just as Curt had predicted. But at the end of that year, Tommy was debt free with a painted house, and we were five thousand dollars in debt with a painted house. The fact that we got ours done faster just didn't seem to matter much in the grand scheme of things. This was one of those life lessons that we have never forgotten. We learned that sometimes it's best to chip away at something a little at a time. It might take a year, or five years, but in the end you'll have accomplished something you can take pride in. Like Tommy and his painted house, you'll know you put your efforts into something that mattered, no matter how long it took you.

Getting out of debt can feel like Curt did that day as he tried his hand at painting our house. "This is too huge! It's going to take forever!" I know that's how we felt as we sat down and, with a yellow legal pad, wrote down all the debts we owed, one after the other. While looking at the list was overwhelming, we knew we had to get it all on the table. Medical debts, credit card balances, car payments, home equity line, student loans we'd carried our entire married life—it all went on the list. And it certainly looked like a mountain of debt. But Jesus said, "I tell you the truth, if you have faith as small as a mustard seed, you can say to this mountain, 'Move from here to there' and it will move. Nothing will be impossible for you" (Matt. 17:20).

We studied the list, discussed the list, and formulated a plan of attack. We would attack the $95,000 of debt the same way you eat an elephant: one bite at a time. We targeted the first debt we'd knock out and began to chip away at it with every spare penny we had.

If you're looking to move your money mountain, there are three steps you must immediately take:

1. Create a budget.
2. Start giving to your church, or reaffirm your commitment to do so.
3. Cut expenses everywhere you can.

While these steps might not make total sense in today's world, they completely add up in God's economy. You might be thinking, *Give money away when I don't have it to begin with? But that makes no sense!* We've learned from experience that this is an essential part of the process. We tried to get out of debt before and made no headway whatsoever, suffering setbacks that threw us off track. Adding giving to the equation balanced it in a supernatural way. It was only after we did it God's way that we saw a difference. We've lived out the idea that you simply cannot outgive God. Though we resisted this truth for years and years, it was only when we began giving in freedom and love that we experienced God's healing hand on our finances in a significant way. We had to discover the difference between *fearful* giving and *cheerful* giving. Fearful giving is obligatory giving that is accompanied by a very real fear that we won't have enough left to take care of our needs. Cheerful giving is joyful and is accompanied by a trust in God to meet all of our needs, even when the numbers don't add up.

Curt

Marybeth and I grew up in church, and all of our lives we've heard that we're supposed to tithe ten percent. Even as newlyweds with very meager incomes, we understood that we should be giving part of our money to our local church. But we were so deeply in debt and I was so afraid of not being able to care for my family that I resisted any effort to tithe. I tightly wrapped my arms around what I called "mine." Under the surface, I was dealing with a lot of emotions. I was scared of not being able to feed my family. I was struggling with anger directed toward God for not rescuing me from our serious financial problems. Every time the subject of giving came up at church, I would get upset and felt like the pastor was using guilt to manipulate me into tithing to the church. There were times when I would write out a check, but only grudgingly, regretting it the moment I dropped it into the offering plate. I was a fearful giver.

It took many years, but God patiently helped me learn that there is deep joy in giving. I began to internalize that everything in my life— including my money, my marriage, my family, my house, even my job—belonged to God. He wanted to teach me to quit holding my fists in tight little balls and to open my hands, surrendering all of my life, including my money, back to Him. It was a scary realization. I'd look at our budget with a strong desire to give but not have any idea where the money could come from. I'd write out a small tithe check and leave it at the church, but feel torn with conflicting emotions of joy and fear. In my heart I was trying to honor and obey God even though I wasn't sure how my family would make it to the end of the month. The funny thing was we never went hungry, we were always able to pay our bills, and our kids always had clothes. God took care of all the small things I worried about. He helped stretch our finances to cover all of our needs. He taught me to be a cheerful giver.

I began to see giving in a much different light. It became a priority for me. Instead of getting angry trying to fit tithing into our budget, I found joy in looking for every extra dollar I could give back to God. A few years ago, on a Wednesday night after church, a woman I'd been helping learn to play guitar unexpectedly gave me $15. A few weeks prior, to help her out, I recorded a few worship songs on tape so she could hear the chords and the strum patterns. She gave me the money that night as a small token of thanks. What she didn't know was that during the service I'd been talking to God about how tight things had been lately with our budget and how much it hurt to not have anything to bring. After I thanked her and she walked away, I went straight to the offering box and dropped the money in. I left church that night with tears in my eyes, realizing that God hears even our smallest prayers and cares about even our smallest needs. We give to our heavenly Father because He loves us enough not only to give us His Son, but He loves us enough to care for our daily needs.

In the grand scheme of things, all of our money doesn't really amount to much. What I'm learning is that God doesn't care about dollar amounts. Instead, He wants to teach me to trust Him with everything I have in this life, and to honor Him with my giving. Money in our home is still tight, and giving our money back to God is always a sacrifice. What I've learned is that there's a deep joy in honoring God with my giving.

> I have no need of a bull from your stall
> or of goats from your pens,
> for every animal of the forest is mine,
> and the cattle on a thousand hills.
> I know every bird in the mountains,
> and the creatures of the fields are mine.
> If I were hungry I would not tell you,
> for the world is mine, and all that is in it.
> Do I eat the flesh of bulls
> or drink the blood of goats?
> Sacrifice thank offerings to God,
> fulfill your vows to the Most High,
> and call upon me in the day of trouble;
> I will deliver you, and you will honor me.
> Psalm 50:9–15

Marybeth

Most importantly, we learned that the key is to start simply and simply start. By formulating a plan—together—we could move forward, one determined step at a time. We'll go into steps one (creating a budget) and three (cutting spending) in separate chapters, so I want to spend the rest of this chapter focusing on how to formulate a plan of attack.

Our plan of attack came to us in phases.

Phase One: SEE

The first phase began that night shortly before Christmas, when we sat in our parked car for over an hour and discussed what it would look like for us to get out of debt. There in that car, we talked about how important it was for our future and became united in our efforts. This was our SEE (Significant Emotional Event). In order to *see*, you have to have vision. That night, our vision became laser focused. This first phase was an essential element to our plan. Though we didn't realize it at the time, we were laying a foundation that we would stand on in the years to come. This foundation had to be strong and sure, or else it would collapse under pressure. Our commitment level had to be 100 percent: commitment to the plan, commitment to each other, and commitment to the Lord. My advice is don't attempt to move on to phase two unless you've experienced phase one.

If you and your spouse are struggling in any of these areas of commitment, spend time praying, and trust God to unite you in His timing. It can be hard to wait for this to happen, but I've learned that pushing the issue is of no use. This commitment phase will be effective only if the hearts of both parties are fully invested in it. Forcing it to happen is counterproductive. Instead of spending your time nagging, suggesting, manipulating, or whining, spend that time praying for God to move in your marriage and your finances. Cling to the promises in His Word that He does hear the cries of His people. It might not feel like He is moving, but He is.

Phase Two: Plan

The second phase occurred when we sat down and listed all our debts, painstakingly including every one. We accounted for every debt—from the tiniest balance on a children's store credit card to the largest balance on a car that was far from paid for. While it was painful to see that overall balance growing with each entry, it was also strangely exciting. By making a plan, we could see exactly how to move forward. We had something to aim for. We circled that first debt we were going to zero in on and that became our immediate focus. Beginning with the smallest debt gave us a goal that was both realistic and reachable. Paying that debt off would give us a victory sooner rather than later. Then we could build on that victory, based on success and hope. Instead of focusing on how overwhelmed we were by that very large number, we broke it down into doable, incremental goals. Remember the elephant? One bite at a time.

Phase Three: Act

This phase lasts the longest. It's the time to take action and to live out the plan. This phase can drag on from months to years. And, rest assured, there will be times when it seems this phase does nothing but drag on, and we'll discuss how to deal with discouragement in another chapter. In living out the plan, though, it's helpful to have that piece of paper posted or filed somewhere that is easily accessible. As you clear out another debt, you can cross through it with a thick black magic marker. As silly as it sounds, it's rewarding to physically cancel out those debts and see those black lines adding up. Curt actually created a spreadsheet on the computer that allowed him to do the equivalent of this. He could pull up the document and see how far we'd come instead of solely focusing on how far we had to go.

As you pay off one debt, take the money you'd been paying monthly on that debt, add it to the minimum you've been paying toward the next item on your list. In this way you're increasing the amount to put toward paying off balances instead of just paying monthly fees and/or minimums. Dave Ramsey calls this method "the debt snowball." We used to try to target our largest balance, but we only got caught up in despair as we could never seem to reach our goal and ultimately threw our hands up in hopelessness. This simple adjustment of our plan resulted in feeling confident and capable as we experienced quick success.

Phase Four: Maintain

This phase has been long in coming, but as I type this we are finally there. Just a few months ago, we became debt free—except for our mortgage. We paid off $95,000 of debt on one income while providing for six children in about four years' time. That is a God-sized task that we know had little to do with what we did and everything to do with our obedience in whatever God asked us to do.

In phase four we turn the energy and intensity we used to pay off debt toward saving and giving. We'll spend phase four tithing regularly, giving to others, and putting money into a fund that will cover any major setbacks, repairs, or other catastrophic events. This fund should have three to six months of living expenses in it at all times.

Where phases one through three are about struggle and endurance, phase four is about walking in conviction and principles, always remembering the height from which you have fallen. It's about never judging another person who has fallen into the same trap but extending your hand to them with words of encouragement and grace. Phase four is also about asking God for help as you resist the temptation to fall into old habits and ease up on the focus you've had to maintain for so long. In short, phase four is not a time to get lazy! Phase four is about realizing how far you've come—and how easy it would be to go back. It's about making sure you have a continued relationship with God, time in His Word, people you are accountable to, and continued communication about finances with your spouse to ensure that you never again go back the way you came. It's about walking in a wisdom that was hard earned, indeed.

■ STUDY

Read Joshua 3:14–17; Proverbs 29:18; Ecclesiastes 4:9–12; and

Revelation 2:5. Take a few moments to think through why we have included these passages in this chapter. How might God be challenging you to apply them to your life?

■ REFLECT, DISCUSS, PLAN

1. If you're reading this book as a group study, discuss with your group what you think the verses above have to do with this chapter.

2. Isaiah 28:10 says, "Do and do, do and do, rule on rule, rule on rule, a little here, a little there." In this verse, the people are making fun of the prophet Isaiah, poking fun at what they have determined is Isaiah's simplistic requests of them. And yet sometimes all God asks of us is to make the smallest steps and trust Him with the big outcome. In this way, we'll know the success is only by His doing and none of ours. Can you begin to chip away at your debt "a little here, a little there"? Do you trust God to take your little efforts and multiply them?

■ TAKE ACTION

Have you experienced phase one with your spouse yet? If so, are you approaching your journey as a "cord of three strands" as the verse in Ecclesiastes references? Is God part of this journey for you? Consider buying a cord of three strands from a home furnishings shop and displaying it in some way in your home. Let it serve as a visible reminder of what is necessary for this journey.

Chapter 6

TAKING THE HARDEST STEP

Curt

I recognized the desperation in his voice. A friend had called and was describing how out of control his finances had become. He and his wife were behind on their bills, including their house payment, and weren't sure how to get current with everyone. Creditors were calling his house and making demands for payments. I asked him some basic questions about his living expenses and debt payments, and after a moment of uncomfortable silence, he said, "You know, to be honest, I'm not really sure." When I pressed for more information about how he and his wife prepare a budget he admitted that they'd never developed a spending plan and were living chaotically month to month.

Having an accurate budget, or spending plan, has been the key to Marybeth and I cleaning up our financial mess. Over the years, we've learned a lot about what works with budgets and what causes more problems. As I've counseled other couples who are struggling with their finances, I've seen that they either don't have a budget prepared, or have one but aren't using it regularly. For these families, operating the finances is a haphazard event with little thought given to the amount spent on things like gas, groceries, clothes, or eating out. Even worse, there is little, if any, healthy communication about money between husband and wife. One spouse is struggling to juggle the day-to-day expenses of the home and experiencing a high level of stress trying to keep up. The other spouse is disengaged, hoping all the problems will go away. When I'm sitting down face-to-face with a couple in this situation, one of the first things I notice is the amount of tension that has filled the atmosphere of the home.

Marybeth and I lived this way for many years. We didn't have a budget that was an accurate representation of our monthly expenses. We had no healthy communication about our finances. I lived in constant fear that our house of cards was going to collapse, and let that fear turn me into a control freak about money. Poor financial management created serious emotional issues in our marriage that Marybeth and I had to address before we could move into a deeper relationship and begin managing our money together. It was during this time in our marriage that we began to understand the importance of working together to develop and maintain an accurate budget.

Build a Foundation for the Future

One Sunday in church our pastor shocked the congregation by saying that God shouldn't be first on our list of priorities. "As a matter of fact," he said, "God shouldn't even be on the list." After a pause for nervous laughter, he went on to explain his statement. His point was that God should be the *foundation* upon which we build all the areas of our lives. God's not first on our list; He's the paper that we write the list on. God's not a "to do" that we check off after we've finished our quiet time and read our Bible, but a constant presence with whom we have continual interaction. Our relationship with our heavenly Father affects every aspect of our lives from the time we rise up in the morning until we fall asleep exhausted at night.

An analogy can be made to the family budget. Developing a plan for how money is going to be spent isn't the first step in fixing your family's finances; it's the foundation upon which you must build your finances. Before you can tackle your debts, your giving, your college funds, or your retirement, you have to develop an accurate budget that not only gets you from pay period to pay period, but helps you plan for your future.

Difficulties

The company I work for recently underwent an organization change. I was given a new role that included overnight travel to different offices in my region. I'm the kind of person who's energized by meeting and working with many different people and finding ways to improve our company, so I look forward to the trips. After a few months of overnight travel, however, I found three things that I struggle with when I have to leave town. One is getting organized for my trip. I put planning and packing off until the last minute and then scurry around like a madman afraid that I've forgotten something I'll need. The second is procrastination. Although I enjoy the excitement of getting to work in different locations, I don't like leaving home and have a hard time getting started on my journey. I know how tough it is to be away from my wife and kids, and I put off leaving until the last minute. The third thing I struggle with is the trip itself. Even with good podcasts on my iPod or good books to read, traveling is exhausting. My body just doesn't do well sitting for long periods of time. Whether I am flying or driving, halfway into a long trip, I'm going stir-crazy.

These are the same three problems people have developing a budget. The hardest but most important part of the budget journey is getting organized. It's imperative that a husband and wife work together to get an accurate picture of their income and expenses over a longer time period than just the next paycheck; they should be able to write out all of their income for at least three months. "Income" would include any form of net payment (take-home pay) into the family's finances, including commission checks and part-time income. Expenses would include these general categories:

1. *Giving*: regular items that the family gives money to such as tithing to their local church, supporting a child through Compassion and giving to parachurch ministries
2. *Savings*: money needed for an emergency fund and investments
3. *Living expenses*: payments to power, water, cable, phone, or insurance, as well as expenses for food, gas, toiletries, restaurants, or any other category where there is regular spending
4. *Variable expenses*: fluctuating expenses like clothing for the kids, medical costs, or yearly taxes
5. *Debts*: payments made for credit cards, car payments, student loans, old medical bills, or any other company where money is owed

The second problem people have living off a monthly budget is getting started. Just as I procrastinated leaving home because of the emotional and physical drain of traveling, Marybeth and I put off developing and living on a budget. We were intimidated by the amount of time we'd have to devote each week to update and maintain the paperwork and the bills. We also knew that the detailed monitoring entailed in operating a budget would take a level of emotional energy we weren't accustomed to. The daily challenge of juggling work, marriage, and kids was tiring enough without adding the pressure of continually measuring our finances against a budget.

The third, and possibly the most exhausting, part of budgeting is going the distance. One of the most frustrating things about traveling is thinking about how far it is to my destination— "Are we there yet?" Similarly, living on a budget isn't something you do for a few months and then stop. Living on a budget is a lifelong commitment. When Marybeth and I first created a spending plan for our finances, we saw, perhaps for the first time, how long it was going to take to pay off all our debts. Many times as I'd write out all of my family's income and expenses for three or four months, I'd feel extremely discouraged. The financial state of our lives seemed overwhelming.

Benefits

As tough as it was getting started, having a plan on paper has been the key to changing the way Marybeth and I manage our money. Having a budget has benefited us three ways. One is that it gave us a common vision. It wasn't easy going through our expenses and finding ways to afford living month to month. We both had to make sacrifices. We'd get frustrated and argue over categories for which we felt we needed more or less money. It was stressful to see all of our debts listed on paper and to talk about how long it would take to pay everything off. But in the end, our budget became a common goal that we could work together to achieve.

Another important benefit was that our budget—our plan for our money—guided our decision making. We began each pay period knowing how every single dollar was going to be spent. We were able to manage the stress of variable expenses like clothes for the kids and annual tax bills. By creating and living on a budget, Marybeth and I were better prepared for the unexpected, like the dishwasher breaking or a car needing repair. And because all the numbers were in front of us on paper, we could regularly measure our spending and keep our finances in balance.

The most significant thing that having a budget did for our marriage was significantly decrease the tension and the fights we had about money. Before we started using a budget to plan and operate our finances, Marybeth and I would fight whenever things went wrong—and they usually did! We'd bounce a check, blame each other, and not speak for days. God's desire is that we become one, to be a unified team fighting together through the difficulties of life. But without a budget, when things got tough, we became each other's enemy and fought over who was wrong and who was right. Today, by having a "third party" in the room called "budget," Marybeth and I are able to quit fighting each other. A budget lets us work together to solve problems.

Start Today

The first step in preparing a budget is getting organized. I'm the detail-minded person in our marriage and the one who actually pays the bills, keeps the records, and balances the checkbook. As Marybeth and I began to create an accurate budget, we had to list all of our incoming and outgoing money as accurately as possible. While the income side was generally pretty easy to figure out, the outgoing side took some time. I knew how much we needed to pay our regular bills like credit cards and utilities, but knew little about how much to budget for groceries and other living expenses. Marybeth and I also spent a lot of time going over the sporadic expenses that come up over the course of the year like kids' clothing, car maintenance, and money for school activities. I found that our monthly expenses could be divided up into five main categories: giving, savings, expected bills, variable expenses, and debt payments.

Regular giving includes any money that is donated on a monthly basis to church, local charity, or other national foundation. Savings would be money set aside on a regular basis for an emergency fund, saved for a child's college fund, money invested into a 401K savings plan, or any other money used to invest. The category for expected bills includes payments to companies such as power, phone, cable, water, and insurance companies.

Variable expenses are the hardest to plan for. The best example of variable expenses is clothing for the family. Keeping our family of eight in clothes can get expensive. Because we typically buy clothing seasonally, the cost becomes a variable expense that we have to plan for each month. At the beginning of each year, Marybeth and I will estimate how much we'll need to spend for each child for the year, add it all up, and then divide by twelve. Each month we'll set aside that amount into our savings account. Then, when a new season arrives and we need to shop, or when we find a great deal on clothes, the money is available. Other variable expenses include maintenance for cars, insurance premiums that are paid annually or biannually, and tax bills paid on an annual basis. Marybeth and I also use this process to save for expensive items like pieces of furniture we need. Each year, we add up the total annual cost for all of these items, divide that figure by twelve, and save that amount every month. If, for example, we want to buy a new dining room table and chairs that costs $2,400, we'll put $200 in savings for twelve months until the money is saved. Then, we'll go pay cash for the furniture.

Last but not least in the budget is payments made on debts to companies. This category includes items such as car loans, student loans, credit cards, and all debts you're working to pay off. The goal of any good budget is to pay off all your debts so that this category has nothing in it!

Once you've determined how much money comes in and goes out each month, you must develop a system to keep track of all of your expenses every single pay period. Every time I get paid, I list all of our family's income and then start subtracting the money I'm going to give, the money I'm going to save, the money I'll need for bills, the money for variable expenses, and the money I'll need for debt payments. Every single dollar listed as income gets put in one of the expense categories before the pay period begins. If I'm any less organized, money gets wasted on things we didn't really need, and before the pay period is up our family runs short in critical categories like groceries or gas. I've also learned that we can't start mixing up our spending. If, for example, Marybeth or I take money from what's allotted for groceries and use it to eat out, the grocery category will run short and we'll be eating a lot of peanut butter and jelly at the end of the month. The important thing is to stick to what you've created on paper.

So, spend time getting organized and developing your plan:

1. List your income.
2. List your monthly expenses.
   + Giving
   + Savings
   + Expected payments

- ◆ Variable expenses
- ◆ Debt payments
3. Decide who will be the "budget administrator" and let that spouse decide what system he or she will use.
4. Work together to develop your spending plan for the next three months.

Communicate

Developing this spending plan can be frustrating and cause tension between a husband and wife as you try to stretch out your income to cover all of your needs. But we've found that it's always less stressful to be proactive and create a plan before the spending starts. Not having a budget and hoping you can make it to the end of the month never works out. Communication between husband and wife, then, is an extremely important part of developing an accurate picture of your household budget.

In developing your plan for managing your money month to month, you need to spend time talking about each category. You also should write out all of the variable expenses you could have over the next year so you know how much to save for them each month. Marybeth and I, for example, go every year to a homeschool book conference and buy our kids' homeschool curriculum. It usually costs about $1,000 for the hotel, gas, food, and books we buy. Because it's a big expense that we can't cover with that month's income, we have to save for the trip every month over the course of the year. A husband and wife have to sit down regularly and talk about all of these kinds of expenses and work them into your monthly cash flow plan.

The friend I mentioned in the opening part of this chapter learned this valuable lesson. He and his wife were living without a plan. They'd gotten into debt and were struggling to pay their bills. The tension had grown so bad between the two of them that they were barely speaking. Sitting down and listing out all their income and expenses helped them develop a budget that stretched every dollar. Every single paycheck was spent on paper before the month began. Their monthly budget became a written contract between the two of them, and they both agreed they would stick to it no matter what. If things came up and they needed to move money from one category to the other to cover a shortfall, they agreed that they'd work together to fix those kinds of problems. When money got tight and the pressure mounted, they were able to focus on the sheet of paper without the fighting that they used to experience.

Because they lived on a budget, they were able to develop a plan not only to get out of debt, but to save six months' worth of expenses in an emergency fund for something unexpected like a job loss or car repair. Instead of reacting month to month as bills popped up out of nowhere, they now have a plan and are prepared. With the stress of money drastically reduced in their lives, their marriage has grown strong. They can talk about money without fighting. They're learning to be good managers of God's money, and for the first time in their marriage, are able to help others in need.

It all started with a man reaching out for help and a husband and wife taking control, developing a plan, and sticking to it.

See Faith in Action

If all of this sounds new to you, don't worry. You're not alone. Marybeth and I didn't understand any of these budgeting principles when we got married. We were just young kids who knew we wanted to share a life together. Now, after meeting with many other couples, I think the same is true of most marriages. My sister and her husband, Jennifer and Mark, would agree. Like most Americans, they grew up thinking that car loans, credit cards, and student loans were *normal*. They had never developed a monthly budget and had no financial plan guiding their decisions. Mark had graduated from Duke University and was a minister in the Methodist Church. Jennifer was in medical school and thought she wanted to pursue a career as a doctor. Like most Americans, they were using debt to pay their way through school, and then expected to use a well-above-average income to pay everything off. But after having a little girl, Jennifer realized that in her heart she wanted to be at home raising her kids. Jennifer shares her story:

When Mark and I first thought about my staying at home, we were convinced we wouldn't be able to afford it. We'd never lived on a budget before. But at my core, I knew I wanted to be a full-time mom. We were committed. Then God gave me the insight that if I was smart enough to get through college and most of med school, then I was smart enough to figure out how to live on one income. I read Larry Burkett's book Women Leaving the Workplace *and then got to work on our budget. I tracked every one of our expenses for a month and went from there. We cut our expenses, cut off our cable, committed to the full tithe, and worked on reducing our credit card debt. It was a lot of work, but I was motivated because I knew I wanted to stay home.*

Every month, we worked our plan, relying on full disclosure about expenses and income. We have equal access to our accounts and our own budgeting information. I'm the detail person in our marriage, so I balance the checkbook. But I ask for Mark's help, just to keep up. It eases my mind to know that he sees the numbers on a regular basis. We also reevaluate our budget every couple of months to make sure we have a handle on where our money's going and where we want it to go.

Another insight is that we rely on God's provision—not on my husband, or his employer—for our family. We are cared for by the hand of God. God gives and God takes. Blessed be the name of the Lord! If there is a season of want, we look to God for direction. If we have a season of plenty, we ask God how He would like us to use it. And in all things we say "Thank you."

Our student loans have been a major source of anxiety and stress. Many times I've thought, If only we didn't have this debt, we could be financially comfortable instead of having to keep such a tight rein on every expense. *But God has used our loans to show us His faithful provision. Following Crown Financial Ministry, we committed ourselves to getting out and staying out of debt. So once we paid off our credit cards, we rolled that money over to the smaller student loan and accelerated our payments. No matter what else happened financially, we reserved that money for the student loan.*

Despite real financial hardship, we kept up our payment schedule and tried to trim our budget in other ways. Then, without our expecting it, God gave us, through an inheritance, the entire amount we needed to pay off the smaller loan, five years ahead of schedule. So with the extra money we're accelerating our payments on my very large medical school loan. Right now, I plan on paying it off about ten years ahead of schedule.

Living on a budget isn't easy. I find it requires constant vigilance. We're always weighing our priorities and checking up on our expenses before we make a purchase. But I find that if I slack off, we'll feel it before the month is over.

In short, this whole budgeting thing is a marathon. And we trust God for the grace to run it.

■ STUDY

Read Proverbs 8:10–11; 21:20; Ecclesiastes 4:9–12; and Luke 14:28–30.

■ REFLECT, DISCUSS, PLAN

1. Do you and your spouse have an accurate spending plan that you use month to month? Why or why not? If no, how could you get started? Who would be the detail-minded person in your marriage who could pay the bills and balance the checkbook? If you do have a plan, are there problems with your current process that you could work on as a team to improve?
2. Proverbs 21:20 teaches us that we should live on less than we make. It took years for Marybeth and I to learn that our spending needed to match our income, not exceed it. What are ways that you could reduce your spending to help your family live on less than you make?
3. What financial vision do you have for your family? What two-, five-, and twenty-year goals are you trying to achieve? How would having a detailed spending plan help you achieve those goals?

4. Jennifer made special note that God's provision is a central factor in their budgeting decisions. How can you make this insight part of your future budgeting decisions?

■ TAKE ACTION

If you've never used a budget in the past, start the process of learning about your monthly expenses. Write down and keep a running total for the next 30 days of how you and your spouse spend your money. Sit down and talk about each of the expense categories mentioned in this chapter, using as much time as necessary to determine how much should be budgeted for your needs. Be as specific as you can with items such as groceries, eating out, gas, toiletries, etc. Go online to www.daveramsey.com or www.crown.org and download free budgeting forms to use as you begin to develop your plan.

Chapter 7

LEARNING TO
LIVE ON LESS

Marybeth

Have you ever had a frozen blended coffee drink? They're dangerously high in calories, not to mention expensive and really yummy! Curt and I got hooked on them several years ago. Many, many nights—okay . . . I confess it was every night—Curt and I ventured out after dinner on warm summer evenings and indulged ourselves in some frozen coffee goodness. One day Curt came to me with a grim look on his face, waving a piece of paper. "I need to show you something," he said. He laid down the paper, which had a column of figures written on it. At the top was the cost of two of these drinks, multiplied by the number of nights we were getting them per week, multiplied by four weeks in a month, multiplied by twelve months in a year. His calculations had resulted in a terrifying discovery. We were on track to spend literally hundreds of dollars per year—enough to buy clothes for a whole season for all of our children, and that's saying a lot—on coffee drinks that were enjoyed for mere minutes, and then forgotten. We were sad to give up our habit, but chose to limit the pilgrimage to special occasions like date nights.

This discovery was just one of many we made once we started taking a serious, intentional look at where our money was going. We discovered some areas that absolutely had to be cut. Just like the coffee drinks draining our finances over time, so would many other unnecessary expenses. At first this meant that we cut out cable television. We didn't pay for high-speed Internet but made do with dial-up. We stopped printing things from our home printer. We shopped around for the most inexpensive life insurance and car insurance policies. Not a stone was left unturned as we vigorously—and at times viciously—cut things out that were not mandatory for our survival.

Think *Survival*

Survival is a key word. When you make the decision to do whatever it takes to get out of debt, you have to go into survival mode. You have to live without a great many things that the rest of the world takes for granted. Why? Because you need that freed-up money to make your payments and to chip away at your debt. This lifestyle is not about pleasure and luxury. It's about sacrifice and bare minimums for a time.

The other day the wife of one of our pastors was at our house when we were talking about a popular kids' show on cable television. She sheepishly confessed to everyone there that she wasn't familiar with the show because they didn't have cable TV. She and her husband are living off one income with a pastor's salary and they've had to make cuts for her to stay home. "Good for you," I said. I know from experience that their lives will be all the better for it. It's not easy to be different—not to have all the little extras we see others enjoying—but it does serve a greater purpose. In the end, the peace of staying out of debt far outweighs the momentary happiness of those little extras in life. Sometimes this peace requires us to simply eliminate spending everywhere we can.

Eliminate Spending

Here are suggestions based on things we've eliminated in our household:

1. Think through services you utilize. Haircuts, dry cleaning, house-keeping, gym membership, nail care, and other indulgences can either be stretched out longer or eliminated altogether.
2. Limit what you do for your children. This might mean stopping allowances, postponing some seasons of sports, temporarily halting piano or dance lessons, skipping elaborate birthday parties, and meeting only their most basic needs and not their wants for a time. Put your family's financial future ahead of those things your children will probably not remember.
3. Along these same lines, consider how much clothing your children need. Do they really need as many pieces of clothing as they have? Can they really wear it all? Even if you buy it at yard sales or on deep discount, you can still end up with way more clothing than any one child needs. Stop yourself from buying too much and decide on what is a good amount of outfits per child. Then stick with that—no matter how cute or how cheap that little sweater is!
4. If your children go to private school, have a tough conversation about other options. This is also true for preschool and mother's morning out programs for little children. We all like having a break, but is that the best use of your money at this time? As for private school, that's an important decision that each couple must come to through prayer and discernment. Look into magnet schools, charter schools, university model schools, or even homeschooling—if that's where God leads you—as an alternative to the high costs of private education. Without both preschool and private school tuition, that freed-up money can go a long way toward paying off debt.
5. Take a look at the name brands you buy and eliminate what you could live without. This includes food brands, clothing brands, or any other brand-name product. Consider buying less-expensive brands, store brands, or shopping at consignment stores to get the same brands for less. This can save quite a bit of money once you get past the mind-set of having certain names on your athletic equipment, shoes, and bags.

6. Really think through how much gas you're using. Eliminate gas waste by carpooling, reducing activities, or simply not going certain places. Take a few moments to map out your route before leaving to run errands so that you can maximize your gas mileage by not backtracking.

7. Pets are great, but they're expensive! It might be necessary to cut back on professional grooming, treats, toys, collars, and equipment. And especially don't get any new pets until your financial situation is much more stable.

8. Look into bundling services or restructuring your billing. We bundled our cable, Internet, and phone for considerable savings. It's worth a phone call to your providers to discover where you might be spending unnecessary money. You can also shop the competitors.

9. If you use a cell phone, it might be time to eliminate your home phone. We've never done this because we get terrible cell phone reception in our home. But many of our friends have had good results with this option.

10. Stop eating out. Make a restaurant meal an occasional, anticipated treat and start eating at home.

11. Evaluate whether warehouse clubs are really saving you money. If you only have a small amount to spend, sometimes it's easier on your monthly budget not to buy such large amounts at once—not to mention finding storage space for all that food. We feed a family of eight from a regular grocery store, don't own an extra freezer, and have a normal-sized pantry. It can be done.

Shop Wisely

Another way we've lived on less is to find ways to save money in areas that you can't eliminate—like food or clothing—but can learn to shop wiser and enjoy savings as a result. Here are some ideas that have saved money for us:

1. Make a menu plan each week. I can't stress this enough. I know firsthand that the temptation to eat out goes way up when mom doesn't know what's for dinner. By creating menus, you can make a list of everything that you need to make those meals, and then shop, using that list each week. I post our menus on the side of the refrigerator in no certain order. Then each morning I choose something to prepare from the list. That way I know if I need to start a meal in the slow cooker or pull something out to thaw ahead of time. I can also do little things to pull the meal together during the day so there isn't a mad rush right at dinner time. Once you get used to this system and build up a repertoire of meals, it really requires minimal thought and minimal effort.

2. When you make a menu, pull out the grocery store ads or go online to find them at whatever stores you frequent. Some great Web sites for this are listed below. I use these ads to make my menu. If ground beef is on sale that week, for instance, I know we're having spaghetti, tacos, or sloppy joes. This saves a lot of money!

3. Coupons work for some people. Clipping coupons is a great way to save 40–60% on your grocery bill. There are some folks who have made "couponing" a lifestyle! I've found that they're hard to keep up with and really only tempted me to buy things I didn't normally buy. I've given myself freedom from coupons and resolved to save that money in other ways. Feel free to do the same if coupons stress you out. An Internet search on the word "couponing" turns up many articles for those who want to learn more.

4. Shop Craig's List or Freecycle.com for furniture. We've bought several nice pieces from Craig's List, which is a free listing of a variety of items. Most of our furniture has, in fact, been either given to us or bought secondhand. (Use caution with Craig's List, however, as there are some questionable elements on the site that should be avoided.)

5. Determine a system for hand-me-downs if you pass clothing

along from one child to the next. If clothing is not organized, labeled, and easy to get to, it serves no purpose and only creates more mess. Hand-me-downs are a huge savings if you make use of them.

6. Along those same lines, buying ahead for the next year is a great idea when stores drastically mark down end-of-season clothing. I used to do this faithfully until it simply got too overwhelming and storage became a problem.

7. Consider bartering for services you normally use. My very creative friend Paige bartered for her daughters' dance lessons for several years. She cleaned the dance studio in exchange for their dance lessons. All it took was simply asking the owner of the studio to reach an agreement that lasted for years and was mutually beneficial.

8. Set up all your bills to be paid online. This saves you money on stamps and many institutions offer a small savings for paying online. It's also convenient because you can request changes and monitor your billing details and account balances by creating an account.

9. Look for creative ways to buy things that you *have* to buy. I have to buy curriculum, for instance, because we homeschool. I've found that, through shopping used sales, going to warehouse sales, using teacher discount cards, making use of the Internet as a resource, and borrowing books from the library, I've been able to homeschool inexpensively. Ask people who are involved in the same things that you are how they've saved money. You'll glean little tricks of the trade that will save you tons of money through the years.

10. Along those same lines, use the library. Our system is wonderful, and I often make use of their hold system, requesting books I want to read and learning to wait instead of spending a lot of money on books I will most likely read only once. I think this is especially true of fiction books, as nonfiction books are often kept for reference.

11. Be smart about buying gifts. Christmas, birthdays, and other special occasions can be real budget busters if you don't play it smart. I've learned to pick up things at warehouse sales and to take advantage of coupons and sale items when buying gifts. For the longest time, I always used the Michael's 50-percent-off coupon and bought birthday gifts there. They have craft kits that make great gifts.

12. Consider how much money you spend on vacations. My friend Lindsey and her family had planned a trip to Disney World but, after looking at their budget, decided something closer to home would be a better way to go. They planned a trip to another amusement park just an hour from home and shortened the length of their trip. Their decision saved them money on gas, hotel, and overall costs but without shorting themselves on family time. Their kids still got to ride rides, eat dinner out, sleep in a hotel, and store away some great family memories—to the tune of several hundred dollars in savings! I thought Lindsey's idea was a great reminder of how we can be big on fun and still small on costs.

13. A number of money-saving Web sites offer tips to save money in your area. Here's a list of my favorites:
    + eHealthInsurance.com: allows you to compare rates and coverage of many different companies
    + LongTermParking.com: clip coupons for most airports in the country
    + CityPass.com: offers discount passes for big city events
    + Citysearch.com: lets you in on free things to do in major cities
    + Kidseatfree.com: a state-by-state list of restaurants where kids eat free
    + The Dollar Stretcher (stretcher.com): provides tons of money saving links, articles, and information in one convenient place
    + Dealking.com, Dealzconnection.com, and Dealcatcher.com: all are sites that offer links to a collection of the best deals

online, with categories for just about everything you could need

* SecretShopper.com: apply to become a mystery shopper and get free stuff
* SideStep.com: searches all the travel sites so that everything is in one place when you're looking for the cheapest airline ticket, rental car, or hotel
* CouponMom.com: helps you organize coupons and maximize savings by eliminating the need for clipping
* TheGroceryGame.com: tracks trends in pricing to help consumers know when prices are at their lowest (small fee)
* mygrocerydeals.com: tells you what's on sale this week at your favorite grocery stores
* CountingtheCost.com: resources for living simply, frugally, and purposefully

Generate Income

A final way we've learned to live on less is to generate more income based on the resources and abilities we have. While this is technically living on more, it's part of the process of taking stock of your home and your family's situation. As we looked at everywhere we could cut and got creative about saving money, we became much more money conscious. We found that we could be doing more to generate income. For us, this meant not giving away so much of our time. We have nothing against volunteering—and we do still volunteer for our church and our local community theater, not to mention the ministry I'm with and through Curt's financial counseling. But when you're in debt you have to be strategic as to how you spend your time.

We took a detailed look at what we had to offer and determined that it made the most sense for me to get serious about freelance writing. I have a degree in writing but I was fearful about putting myself "out there" and setting myself up for rejection. But when you're drowning in debt, something happens to your courage. So I started small and began building from there. While I've never made big money from writing and speaking, I am making more than when I used to do no outside work. And every bit of that money has gone toward paying off debt and helping our family out of financial trouble. It's a great feeling to contribute in that way.

While you might not be a writer, you can do something. I believe that anyone reading this book has an area of expertise, a service you do in a unique way, or a talent you can use to generate additional income. Whether it's baking your famous banana nut muffins and selling them to the local café or cleaning houses better than anyone else or organizing people's space for them, you can contribute something. Many women care for children in their homes. If you don't want to be tied down as a full-time day-care provider, consider offering busy moms a drop-in service so they can run errands. I know many women feel like they already run a service like this for their friends—for free! Sit down with your friends and honestly explain to them that your family needs you to contribute financially. And while you'd love to help them out, you're going to have to start charging by the hour to do so. My guess is they'll be happy to help you.

Glynnis Whitwer, author of *Work@home*, says,

> There are four main ways to make money from home: telecommuting, direct sales, a from-scratch home-based business, and buying a home-based franchise. Each one of these is a good fit for a different type of personality, and is dependent upon the personal and professional goals of the individual. A direct sales company might be the best fit for someone who wants all the foundational work done for them. A telecommuting job is good for someone who just wants to work a shift and be done with it. A home-based business is good for someone who is a bit more creative, who wants to learn all aspects of the business and who is willing to do more up front work to market themselves. Even if someone just wants to earn some pocket cash, this will take more work. And finally, a home-based

franchise is a big investment and is more of a career move than just a way to make some extra money to get out of debt.[1]

Glynnis discusses all of this in detail in her book. If working from home is something you're feeling led to do, I highly recommend adding her book to your reading list.

Using examples of people in my own life, here's a list of ways they've made additional money from home:

1. *Start an organizing business.* My friend hired a mom who was naturally organized to come into her home once a week and, over the course of several months, organize some area of her house. For my non-detail-oriented friend, organization is a challenge. Having someone come into her home and show her step-by-step how to do it made all the difference.

2. *Sew!* This is a lost art, so if you can do it, share it. I know many talented seamstresses who have started their own online shops to sell their wares. You can sew curtains, purses, or baby-wearing slings. My friend Gina has a whole business online called Sew Trendi, with her biggest item for sale being very hip-looking slings she sews herself.

3. *Edit from home.* My friend Valerie edits for a curriculum company from home. My friend Bonita edits books for writers who hire her. My sister-in-law just got contacted to edit an e-book before the author launched it on her Web site. All are great opportunities that can be built into more business as these ladies desire to do so.

4. *Start a blog and host ads, provide links that generate income, or write reviews.* This takes a bit of time to build up, but it can be done—as hundreds of bloggers can attest to.

5. *Paint.* I know of two ladies who own thriving craft businesses painting verses on plaques with bright, whimsical designs. These beautiful pieces hang in the homes of many, sharing God's Word and making these women some extra money in the process.

6. *Make jewelry.* My cousin started this as a hobby and it morphed into a business. She markets herself through a Facebook site and has photos of her jewelry posted for people to purchase.

7. *Do Web site or blog design.* My friend (and blog designer) Dawn stumbled into Web site design when a friend asked her to design a Web site to sell hair bows for little girls. Not knowing anything about Web design, she bought books on different design programs and studied them diligently for several months, learning as she went. After she finished that first project, she began applying what she had learned to designing blogs. Slowly orders began to trickle in. When she had three requests in one week, she knew her little business was taking off. Though she started designing mostly for friends, her business has now grown so that she had to go on hiatus just to catch up with all the work! Dawn says that with determination, you can learn to do most anything. She's seen the blessings of her determination as her business has grown and provided more income for her family.

8. *Like photography?* Sell stock photography through an online service or sell prints of photos through a Web site.

9. *Clean homes.* My friend Marie got her start by helping out a friend who owned a maid service. Little by little she began to get her own clients and her business was born. She's now contracted by a realtor who employs her to clean clients' homes for showings. Her business keeps her out of the home while her children are in school, but has her back at home in time to spend afternoons with them.

10. *Become a personal trainer or nutrition counselor.* You'll have to have specific skills, training, and background for this, but it's a service that's needed, and you can set your own hours to work around your family. I know one woman who started a Pilates studio in her home's sunroom and has classes going every day. Clients love the cozy, private atmosphere of her home, and she's able to do something she loves and is passionate about. A neighbor of mine has just run an ad in our neighborhood newsletter,

offering her personal training services. She gets to stay close to home with her children and our neighbors get a reduced price.

11. *Turn your volunteering into a paid position.* Our babysitter just got hired as a paid intern at our church this summer to do the same job she was doing as a volunteer this school year. She was tickled to get the position, and they were relieved to find someone who didn't need to be trained from the ground up. Don't be afraid to let the decision makers where you volunteer know that you'd like to turn your volunteer position into a paid position. In God's timing, you might just work your way into a job.

12. *If you know a lot about the job market, consider offering counseling to people who are out of work or just looking to change jobs.* Many people are entering a job market that is unfamiliar and daunting. Helping them write résumés, learn how to network, and learn how to find jobs in their field is a valuable service.

13. *Look for holes.* Where do you see needs? What do you hear your friends complain about? How can you meet those needs or solve those problems? Keep your ear out and brainstorm solutions. I got an e-mail recently from a woman who's starting an errand business. She charges a fee to busy women who need shopping done, details attended to, or even children picked up. She saw a need and responded to it—then she was bold enough to put it out there and see what happened.

While it's rare to make a living off these things, it is extra money that can be socked into debt or used to pay for a week's worth of groceries. I think the biggest key to generating more income is to be willing to do whatever it takes. If you're looking at your bank account and the numbers simply aren't working, you have to get serious about putting yourself out there in whatever capacity. Curt's friend at work is now delivering pizzas in the evenings so that his wife can stay home with their baby and they can stay debt free. I admire that kind of commitment. Secondly, be willing to tell everyone about what you're doing. Be bold enough to tell your friends, your neighbors, your hairdresser, your

Sunday school class, your small-group members, etc. Don't apologize for it and don't let fear of rejection keep you silent. You never know—that one person you tell might make all the difference. That one conversation or connection might just open some very important doors.

That was certainly the case for Cheryl Sandberg, who built her home business, An Occasional Chocolate (www.anoccasional chocolate.com), on word of mouth and connections made through the Internet. What began as an interest in making homemade truffles grew into a passion, and then into a profitable business. Cheryl was a stay-at-home mom looking to supplement her family's income from home. She dabbled in different streams of income through the Internet for a while—Web design, eBay, and selling used books on Amazon. She says that all of these brought in additional money and helped form a knowledge base she relied on when she launched her business. "In the early days," she says, "I would make about a thousand dollars a month. When you look at how much money you actually get to keep as a mom working outside the home, you really don't have to bring in much to stay home!"

Eventually, Cheryl took a class on making chocolates and began to make truffles, which were delicious and packaged beautifully for gifts. As people saw her product, they wanted her to teach them to do the same thing. "Truffles can be very expensive to buy, but are quite inexpensive to make yourself," she says. "As a stay-at-home mom, I enjoyed helping out my friends who were also stay-at-home moms trying to provide gifts on a budget." The idea was a hit, and word of mouth helped launch a hobby into a business. On the urging of friends and after much prayer, Cheryl took a few thousand dollars and invested it into her growing business. She says, "I threw it all up on a Web site and an eBay site and waited to see what would happen!" The first year her business made $23,000. As she learned more about search engines from a free online class, she was able to generate more traffic. The second year the business made $90,000. "We grew 350 percent that first year!" she exclaims, still marveling at God's blessing on her business.

Cheryl felt it was important that they run the business with no debt, and they've been able to do that from the beginning. Through her business, she's able to pay cash for private school for her children and fun vacations for the family. When we spoke, she was planning a trip to Hawaii. The family is even relocating, just to accommodate the volume of product she must keep on hand for her business. She involves her kids in customer service, packaging, product design, and business basics, and notes this has been a great education for them. Best of all, she says, through her classes and products she's been able to help many moms start home businesses of their own. One mom sells dipped, decorated cookies from home. Another makes truffles as Cheryl does. Another mom got her kids involved and helped them start their own business selling chocolate-dipped Oreo cookies. Seeing her passion passed on to other moms gives Cheryl a great sense of satisfaction. Her business has not just changed her family's life—but the lives of others.

A Satisfying Solution

All this talk about chocolate has made me think about those yummy frozen coffee drinks we used to buy. In our quest to cut expenses, we learned that our love for those drinks didn't have to go entirely unfulfilled. I discovered this recipe, which is pretty close and much less expensive, and we can make it at home. And so Curt embarked on a quest to make a drink that tasted as good as the gourmet coffee shop version. We invited friends over to weigh in their opinion. We congratulated each other on how frugal we were being. And, while I haven't figured out the total cost of one of these drinks, I know it costs us nowhere near hundreds of dollars a year. And we have the satisfaction of finding a solution to giving up one of life's little pleasures. And so, without further ado, here's the recipe. We hope you enjoy making it at your house!

Coffee Shop Frozen Mocha

Mix

¼ cup instant coffee granules
1 cup sugar
1 cup nonfat dry milk powder
1 cup powdered nondairy creamer
1 cup baking cocoa
¼ tsp. salt

Put the coffee granules in a ziplock bag. With a rolling pin, crush coffee granules into a fine powder. Place in an airtight container. Add the sugar, milk powder, creamer, cocoa, and salt; mix well. Store mix in a cool, dry place for up to a year.

To make drinks:

1½ cups crushed ice
½ cup milk
½ cup mix
Whipped cream

In a blender, combine the ice, milk, and mix; cover and process on high until smooth. Pour into glasses and top with whipped cream, if desired. Makes two.

■ STUDY

Read Proverbs 6:6–8; 10:4; and 21:5.

■ REFLECT, DISCUSS, PLAN

1. What area are you most concentrated on right now—cutting expenses, saving money, or generating income?
2. Is this area a daily struggle or is it becoming a lifestyle?
3. Share a personal money-saving example similar to the coffee drink example we described in this chapter.
4. Share a money-making tip that has worked for you. If you'd like to send it to us, you can contact us through our blog at www .marybethandcurt.blogspot.com. If it's a new tip we've never posted, we'll put it on our blog.

■ TAKE ACTION

Have a cheap date night with your spouse. Farm the kids out or put them to bed early. Make a couple of frozen mocha drinks and sit and talk. Share from the heart about where you are, where your spouse is, and any struggles you might be facing. Use the discussion questions from one of these chapters as a conversation starter, and let the conversation flow naturally from that. Use this as a time to celebrate your marriage, your family, and your quest to be debt free. Make this a connection time—something every marriage definitely needs regularly. Be just as vigilant about this time as you are about getting out of debt.

If you're going to begin generating income as a result of this chapter, tell five people this week about your service or product. Pick up the phone, send out an e-mail, tell people in your daily life, or post it on your blog. Get the word out!

Chapter 8

ESTABLISHING NO-MATTER-WHATS

Marybeth

About five years ago, we learned that a new neighborhood was being built in an area of town we loved. People who bought homes in the first phase of development could get a reasonable price. The neighborhood was near our church and near some good friends, so we decided to take a look at it. After touring the model and looking over floor plans, we decided that moving would be a great idea, not to mention a good investment. We reasoned that by buying at a low price, we'd have automatic equity that would pay off in the long run. Not to mention a brand-new, larger home with all the newest conveniences and more square footage for our growing family.

We spoke to a realtor who agreed to sell our home for us and signed a ninety-day contingency plan with the builder. If our house did not sell during that time, we would lose half of our initial deposit but not be obligated to buy the house. We talked it over and felt that the risk of putting our money down was worth it. I remember praying a lot during that time, asking God to show us the way and make it clear if we were to do this. As I was driving the check out to the builder, I came upon a flood that completely blocked the road to the development. I felt God speaking to me at that moment, saying, "Don't take that check." But did I listen? No! I found a detour around the flood and drove on. I was so excited to place that check in the sales agent's hands. As I did, I just ignored that sick feeling that I was going against God.

Well, our old house did not sell in the ninety-day period the builder had agreed to. So we had a decision to make. Risk the entire amount of the deposit and hope our house sold in another ninety days or cut our losses and walk away from the deal entirely. Curt was adamant that we would not risk the rest of our money and that, for whatever reason, God simply did not want us to move into this house. He had His window of opportunity for our house to sell, and it didn't. We needed to take no for an answer.

The problem was, we'd already gone to the builder's design center and chosen gorgeous granite countertops and gleaming hardwood floors. We'd tweaked the design of the home to fit our family's needs, and I'd pictured myself cooking meals while my children occupied themselves in the playroom just off the kitchen. It broke my heart to let that house go. But in the end, I did what Curt thought was best, and we walked away from the deal.

As I sought God on the house issue, I got the feeling that His *no* was for our protection. That really caused me anxiety. Though the house was a good deal, it would still be a stretch for us to afford. We were pushing ourselves to get that house—but we had our sights set on both the investment as well as the increased room. When God closed that door, I had a fear that, while we thought it was a smart move, He knew something we didn't. Sure enough, the very next year Curt's company restructured his pay and we were knocked down into an income bracket that put us near poverty level for about three years. As we struggled with this news and the effects it was going to have on our family, all I could say to Curt was, "Thank goodness we weren't in that other house." Financially, we would have gone under during that time if we'd had that larger payment to juggle.

Oddly enough, Curt's sister eventually moved into that neighborhood, and now when we drive past it, we tell our kids, "That's the house we almost bought." We can even laugh about it now and are relieved that it wasn't God's plan for our family.

This episode in our lives was a great lesson of God's protection in the area of our family finances. As I look back on our desire to get that house, I see that the flooded road was God's way of trying to stop me from losing even the contingency money we lost on our little gamble. But we chalked that up to an expensive lesson on listening to Him. Charging ahead is unwise if you feel that God is telling you *no*. Psalm 139:5 says, "You hem me in—behind and before; you have laid your hand upon me." I've learned to ask Him to hem us in, and then to trust that when He does so, it's for the best. *No* might be hard to hear, but it's necessary at times—even when we want to stick our fingers in our ears and pretend we don't hear Him.

Just after this house incident we became committed to getting out of debt. In the years that have followed, we've become much different people than we were back then. Our values and priorities are different now. I would not put anything ahead of being in tune with God's plans for us and getting out of debt. This commitment takes center stage to all my other desires and plans. It's become part of our "no matter what."

I first heard the term *no matter what* when a group of us went to one of Dave Ramsey's live financial seminars. In the seminar, he talked about teaching his teens to establish no-matter-whats in dating situations. He reasoned that helping a teen walk through their no-matter-whats before they get in certain situations will help them in the heat of the moment. They can stand on the principles they believe in instead of making an emotional decision. After the seminar, I thought about how this applies to other situations in our lives. I think the most successful people in the world are the people who operate under an innate sense of their own no-matter-whats. They aren't tossed about by the waves and influenced by every new teaching they hear. They've laid down their parameters, and function according to them no matter what. As I thought about this concept, I determined to lay out my own no-matter-whats—especially in the area of finances.

For us, our no-matter-whats have centered a lot on getting out of debt—and the sacrifices it will take to get us to true financial freedom. This means we drive old cars—no matter what. Because driving a new(er) car just isn't worth taking on more debt. It means that we stay in our small(er) home, because we simply aren't ready to take on any more house payment until all of our debts are paid off. For us, this has meant living in cramped quarters and finding creative solutions. It means that we eat out less, go to movies less, hire babysitters less, and spend a lot less money on personal desires. It means that when we get a commission check for Curt or our tax return money, we don't sit down and plan that vacation we've been wanting to take. We turn around and chuck every bit of that money into paying something off. It means we put our total debt load up on the wall as a target and get up every morning to throw more darts at it. Our no-matter-whats fuel us when we lose hope and boost us when we get down about our situation. We might not be crazy about the sacrifices we're making, but we're crazy about the idea of one day finally hitting that target.

As a financial counselor, Curt encounters many couples who are at that crossroad—either continuing a life of "whatever," or heading down the path of no-matter-what. Scott and Denise were one couple who'd decided to take the plunge into the life of no-matter-what. They'd reached a place of doing whatever it took to make their finances right and ensure a stable future for their family.

Looking back, they see that God was leading them down a path to much more than they ever expected. When Scott's job transfer landed them in a new town, they did what many couples do and bought the highest priced house they could afford. Denise had received an inheritance from her parents' estate and was proud to invest that money into their beautiful new home, complete with a gorgeous backyard pool for their kids, who swam competitively. While their home was not a source of pride, it was a source of deep emotional connections. Though they felt the pain each month of being stretched to pay the mortgage, they reasoned that the promises of raises and bonuses at Scott's job would eventually make things easier. "We were doing okay then," Denise remembers. "But I just remember wanting to live a little freer. There were other things we wanted to be able to do—like take mission trips or give to our church."

At the end of that first year in their home, Scott learned he would no longer be receiving yearly bonuses. At the end of the second year, he learned that the company was freezing any hope of future raises. Their plan to gain ground over time was quickly cut off, and the hope of breathing easier each month was gone unless some changes were made. As they prayed and asked God for wisdom, they felt God urging them to sell their home. While helping some friends move, Scott discovered a neighborhood on the other side of town that featured homes with the same amount of square footage for a much lower price. He presented the idea to Denise with a plan for them to move, get the equity from their home, and invest in another home for much less money per month. Denise remembers feeling so torn between wanting to breathe easier each month and wanting to keep the home that had become associated with so many precious memories for their family. While Scott could see it in black-and-white, Denise struggled mightily with the decision.

When they called Curt for counsel, he looked over their finances and assured them that, while money would stay tight, they could stay in their home. He told Denise that he recognized what an emotional decision it was, especially for her, and urged them both to pray some more. As she prayed, she felt God asking her, "Which do you love more—Me or the memories?" She knew God was asking her to trust Him and to surrender her house. Her no-matter-what was more spiritual than financial. She had to learn to trust God—no matter what—and to love Him—no matter what. "I felt like Abraham, laying my Isaac down," she says now.

The family did decide to move, with the full support of their children, who were feeling the strain of materialism in their rather affluent area and wanted to move to a new area of town where having stuff wouldn't be such an issue. This was quite a relief for Denise, who'd expected much resistance from them. It turned out that they moved at a perfect time, as they'd just learned that their son—who had been adopted from Liberia—needed to repeat the first grade. The move allowed him a fresh start in a new school. And so, in August, just in time for the new school year, the family moved into their new home. Just one month later, out of the blue, Scott lost his job.

As Denise reflects on that time, she says, "Had we not moved into that house we would have most definitely gone completely under very quickly. As in, overnight." She smiles. "Instead we were able to make it through." While neither Scott nor Denise would lead you to believe their lives were easy during that period, they both remember it being a time of drawing closer to God and to each other. As Denise says, "It turned out to be the sweetest time of unity and bonding. We had really gotten away from praying together regularly, but we recommitted to doing so after Scott lost his job. We knew we needed to seek God's will together, and hear from Him together. I just remember feeling the most incredible peace through the whole time. Had we not been obedient to Him when He laid it on our hearts to move when we did, the whole thing could have turned out a whole lot differently." She adds, "I've walked in His will and out of His will and there's no place I'd rather be than in it. No matter what that means for our family."

God taught Denise and Scott an incredible lesson about listening to Him and being willing to do what He asks. Sometimes He asks us to do something simply for our good; but sometimes in trusting Him and doing the hard things He asks, we're actually enabling Him to protect us from something much worse. Something we can't see coming, but He can.

Resolutions Versus Real Solutions

Too many times, I think we treat our financial decisions like we treat our New Year's resolutions. We might make a halfhearted attempt at doing things right financially, only to fall off the wagon weeks or months into the process. The problem is our resolutions are too lofty and too ambiguous to be lived out. It's like saying, "I am going to lose weight." And yet, that statement in itself does very little to help us actually lose weight. We need a plan. We need to create our no-matter-whats. We have to turn our resolutions into real solutions. Here's a list of ideas on how to do that where your money is concerned:

RESOLUTION: I'm not going to go into credit card debt anymore.
REAL SOLUTION: I'm going to cut up my credit cards and cancel my accounts so I cannot make charges.

RESOLUTION: I'm going to be a better steward of my money.
REAL SOLUTION: I'm going to be accountable to someone and pray before spending money.

RESOLUTION: I'm not going to make impulse purchases.
REAL SOLUTION: I'm going to wait at least three days to make all purchases. If I still want the item after that time, then I'll go back.

RESOLUTION: I'm going to spend less money somehow.
REAL SOLUTION: I'm going to commit to looking for used items before buying the same thing new. I'm also going to cut coupons and only buy things on sale. I'm going to pray for God to provide all my needs—even if it means waiting longer to buy something I really want.

RESOLUTION: I'm going to manage my money better.
REAL SOLUTION: I'm going to take a class at my church or read a book that will help me learn how to manage my money.

RESOLUTION: I'm going to save money.
REAL SOLUTION: I'm going to start a savings account for a specific amount of money per month through my bank or employer.

RESOLUTION: I'm going to keep track of my spending.
REAL SOLUTION: I'm going to create a budget with expense cat-
                   egories to help me see where my money is going.

RESOLUTION: I'm going to stop wasting money.
REAL SOLUTION: I'm going to assess my spending habits and cut
                   out those things that aren't necessary or don't
                   line up with my priorities.

RESOLUTION: I'm going to talk to my spouse about money.
REAL SOLUTION: I'm going to set up a weekly time to go over our
                   calendars and any upcoming expenses. We can
                   also discuss our budget and take a look at our
                   account at that time if needed.

RESOLUTION: I'm going to be debt free.
REAL SOLUTION: I'll make an appointment with a financial coun-
                   selor or read a book to help me map out a plan
                   for getting out of debt.

The old adage, "If you aim at nothing you will probably hit it," is especially true where financial matters are concerned. The above examples of resolutions versus real solutions show the subtle difference between them. To make a resolution into a real solution, you determine exactly what steps you must take to reach your goal. The key to a workable real solution is having measurable parameters paired with an intentional attitude. Curt calls this becoming laser focused. A regular beam of light just shines on an object, but a laser can cut through steel.

The key to being laser focused is to arrive at two different determinations:

1. *There has never been a better time for you to take action.* Acts 17:26b says, "And he determined the times set for them and the exact places where they should live." God has a plan for you,

and He has appointed you to live in this time, in this place, and in this set of circumstances. He has allowed these financial circumstances in your life, and He will provide the means and the wisdom to change them. The time for procrastination and excuses is behind you. Now is the best time for you to take action.

2. *You can't just recognize a need for action, you actually have to move.* Lots of examples in the Bible show people taking immediate action when God called them. My favorite has to be the story of David and Goliath. David faced overwhelming odds, yet he bravely stood to face the giant. Even when others—wiser and older—told him he was crazy, he still stepped up and took his place in the battle. Even though the task looked impossible, he trusted God to do it. He relied on what he had already experienced with God—not on the looming, overwhelming sight of Goliath. First Samuel 17:48 says, "As the Philistine moved closer to attack him, David ran quickly toward the battle line to meet him." As I read this verse, the words "ran quickly" jump out at me. There is no fear in this verse, no hesitation, no pausing to count the cost. The time to move was upon him and he confidently ran into a battle, trusting God to be with him every step of the way.

As we live out our real solutions, they become the no-matter-whats we live by, modeling a lifestyle of conviction and integrity as we do. As we seek to live a life that is pleasing to God—following His principles even when it's hard to do—we grow closer to Him and become more like His Son. God cares about how we manage our money. Jesus talked about money many times in the course of His ministry here on earth. He knew we would need guidance and limits. Go to Him when you're feeling defeated, and lean on Him when the steps you must take appear too difficult. You'll find that He honors those who honor Him, and He is there to help you live out your no-matter-whats, day-by-day, step-by-step.

■ STUDY

Read Psalm 119:101–104; Ephesians 4:14–15; 6:11–12; and James 1:6.

■ REFLECT, DISCUSS, PLAN

1. Are you laser focused? Is your resolve merely a light beam, or is it strong enough to cut through steel?
2. What is the biggest difference between *resolutions* and *real solutions*? Have you struggled with resolutions in the past and felt like a failure? Why do you think determining your real solutions will help you change that?
3. How can your no-matter-whats influence those around you? How are you modeling a lifestyle of conviction that will inspire your children, your coworkers, and your friends to do the same?

■ TAKE ACTION

Write down your no-matter-whats this week. Take several days to journal, think about, and discuss these with your spouse. Above all, pray about them, and ask God to lay things on your heart that He would have you determine as no-matter-whats for your life.

Chapter 9

FACING UNEXPECTED EXPENSES

Marybeth

Life comes at you fast. That's what the commercials say, and that's what we live every day. Every one of us has a story about how one minute life is normal and the next minute life is turned upside down. As I type this, I'm laid up in bed, and have been for more than a week. Last week I was walking into our small-group leader's home for our weekly meeting, laughing and talking with my thirteen-year-old daughter as I carried a freshly baked loaf of delicious-smelling cinnamon bread. Because I was talking to my daughter and not looking where I was going, I stepped into a hole in their newly sodded yard, twisting my ankle and breaking my foot in two places. One minute life was normal, the next minute it was far from normal. I never anticipated being sidelined by life in an instant. And Curt certainly didn't anticipate having to take over for his sidelined wife for six weeks as she was forbidden to walk on her broken foot!

But that's life, right? Filled with changes and setbacks, wins and losses. This is true with expenses as well. Some of those setbacks are bearable and some feel like we won't live through them. Catastrophic medical bills, unexpected legal fees. Things that fall into our laps can blow us off course. It's inevitable that, as we're digging out from debt, unexpected expenses will come along, and they'll leave us feeling like we've taken one step forward and two steps back—making our journey out of debt seem that much longer and, frankly, impossible.

It's easy at these times to throw our hands up and say, "This is never going to work!" It's easy to get discouraged and wonder where God is when these things happen. At times I've wanted to shake my fist at the sky and shout, "Don't You see what we're trying to do? How could You let this happen?" And yet, as we've lived through these experiences, we've learned that even though we may think God isn't aware of our struggles or doesn't care about what we're facing, He does. While He may have allowed it to happen, He doesn't leave us to fend for ourselves. As we walk through trials, we must learn to look for His activity in the midst of them. Curt and I have seen that God takes care of us in five basic ways. He uses His people, His power, His provision, His purpose, and His peace.

His People

Even as I write this, I'm experiencing the love and care of God's people. As we've faced the trial of dealing with a household of six children, a demanding new job for Curt, a book to write, and a house on the market—all with my broken foot—we've been surrounded with offers to bring meals, keep our children, help with housework, and run errands. We've felt the outpouring of God's love through His people. God designed His church to function this way. And as a friend recently reminded me, the church is not a building; the church is people. The church is the community of believers.

Sometimes it can be hard to share what you're facing. Especially in the area of finances. Shame, embarrassment, and pride keep us from opening up and letting others in. We want to be the ones helping others, not asking for help. I know that's true of me! I want to be the one bringing the meal instead of receiving it. Our tough exterior hides the weaknesses and doubts we carry inside. We want the world to think we have it all together, that we need no one. And yet God created us to need fellowship with others. He designed us to live in community.

When our son was born with a birth defect that required years of specialized medical care costing thousands of dollars, a man in our church asked us if there was anything we needed. Instead of being honest about our situation, we laughed it off, shrugging our shoulders and making jokes about getting by "somehow." God led this man to see through our act and he invited Curt to meet with him later that week. As they sat down, the man leaned across his desk and squinted at him. "I have a friend who wants to remain anonymous," he told Curt. "He'd like to help you. If you'll tell me how much you need, I'm prepared to write you a check on his behalf. But son," he nailed Curt with level a gaze, "you're going to have to tell me what it is you need." The time for hemming and hawing was long past. Curt learned a valuable lesson in that moment about the value of asking God's people for help. There is praying and asking God, but there's also the value of allowing His people to be the answer to that prayer.

Sometimes God uses people to open doors and sometimes he uses them as roadblocks to keep us from making mistakes. Whether through an accountability partner who questions us about a bonehead decision, or a fellow believer who takes a stand, we sometimes need others to step in and stop us from going down the wrong path. We had this happen years ago when we struggled with the urge to regularly replace cars. We never took into account that one day we should actually pay off a car. We merely compared the monthly payments between our current car and a new one. As long as we could afford the monthly payment, we felt that we could afford the car. It's sad to say that we really didn't look at the total price, nor did paying it off ever come up in our decision-making process. We simply wanted what we wanted. Consequently, we traded cars every couple of years.

When our friend John became the manager of a local Ford dealership, we went to him whenever we wanted to buy a new vehicle, figuring he'd give us the best deal. We went to him on three separate occasions to "trade up." On all three occasions, John talked us out of buying the car and showed us the value of staying in what we had. He overlooked a potential sale in favor of steering us down the right path. We were so naive about such things, we didn't even realize what he was doing at the time. We just knew that he wasn't "very aggressive," as we called it.

Years later, I saw John at an event and thanked him for protecting us from taking on more debt than we needed to and keeping us from getting in more financial trouble. He humbly shrugged his shoulders and said, "Well, I just knew you guys had some things to learn. I couldn't sell you a car knowing that wasn't the best thing for your family." God used John's beliefs and integrity to keep us from strapping yet another millstone around our own necks. To this day, I'm grateful for John's foresight and character and that God led us to him for help rather than to someone who would have taken advantage of us. We should never hesitate to tell people what they don't want to hear, or steer them in the right direction if that's what we feel God is leading us to do. We might make the most difference by saying *no* to someone instead of saying *yes*.

His Power

Because we can't see God, it's easy to lose sight of who He is. It's easy to forget how powerful God is, how limitless His resources are, and how far-reaching His vision is for us. It's easy to minimize what He can do for us because our vision is so minimal. In doing that, though, we're limiting His power in our lives. It's up to us to fling open the door to our lives and our money. To give Him limitless access instead of limited access. To say with our words and with our actions, "I trust You, God, to bring about the best for me. Even when I can't see it." To trust His power, and not rely on our own.

We're not the only ones who've been tempted to rely on power other than God's. Even King David—a man God called "a man after his own heart" (1 Sam. 13:14)—lost sight of God's power and allowed Satan to incite him to take a census (1 Chron. 21:1–4). Satan convinced David that he had a better chance at victory if he knew the number of soldiers in Israel. More than that, he got David's attention focused on worldly things and off God. The census "demonstrated David's reliance on numbers of warriors rather than on God."[1] David put more stock in the power of earthly warriors than in God's power at work in his life.

It's likely that all of us have turned to numbers as our comfort—trusting what we can see over what we can't. This is especially true where money is involved. We go to spreadsheets and account balances for comfort, taking our cues about the state of things by the numbers we find there. Meanwhile an all-powerful God is saying, "Just look to Me."

We can learn from David's lesson and live our lives accordingly. In Psalm 20:6–7 David writes, "Now I know that the LORD saves his anointed; he answers him from his holy heaven with the saving power of his right hand. Some trust in chariots and some in horses, but we trust in the name of the LORD our God."

His Provision

One of my favorite stories of God's provision in our lives isn't exactly biblical in scope. It's just a simple, little example of how much God cares for us individually, and how He attends to the details of our lives. We'd returned home to North Carolina from our six-month stint in Wisconsin. It was early in our marriage and money was, as always, very tight for us. We definitely knew the meaning of the phrase "more month than money." One day I realized that we literally had no money left in the account and three more days before Curt got paid. To make matters worse, we were out of groceries. I felt like crying as I stood in front of the empty refrigerator. Instead of having a good cry, I said a prayer, reasoning that seeking God would do a lot more for our circumstances.

Not long after I finished praying, I was upstairs in our bedroom, sorting through some books. As my hand fell on one of the books, I felt an urgency to open it. It was a book on pregnancy I'd loaned to a friend I met in Wisconsin who was pregnant with her first child. I'd reached out to this young mom-to-be because I knew how she felt, navigating new territory in a new marriage. We left much of our son's baby furniture with her instead of moving it back to Charlotte. We knew that this couple was struggling financially like we were and could use the things our son had outgrown.

I opened the book, remembering my friend and wondering how she was doing with her new daughter. As I flipped through the pages, I saw an envelope tucked between them. I'd had this book for several months without even thinking about opening it. Why would I? I didn't need it. Except that God answered my prayer by prompting me to pick it up. In that envelope was a note from my friend, thanking me for giving her the furniture and baby things. And with the note was $25 with an apology that it wasn't more to cover the value of the things we'd given them.

But it was just enough to buy groceries for the next three days.

I flew downstairs waving the check and explaining to Curt what had happened. God had answered my prayers with supernatural provision. God may as well have dropped that money right out of the sky! I learned that day that no need is too small, and we can trust God to provide in the most unexpected ways. In the years to come, I relied on this personal example of God's love and concern for us whenever we faced trials.

My friend Jessica was told by her doctor that she must be confined to bed rest for the remainder of her third pregnancy. At that time she was three months pregnant, so that meant six months of bed rest. As she came home to her little children, ages three-and-a-half and one-and-a-half, she wondered how her household would function without her for that long. She knew that they would all definitely need help. Yet they had no extra money to hire help, and she knew that her friends could be expected to do only so much. When someone at church recommended a homeschool girl who'd be able to nanny three days a week, they hired her—even though they still didn't know where the money would come from.

Instead of fretting about the future, they trusted God to provide, and gave Him the situation in prayer. Just a few weeks after the nanny came to work for them, Jessica's husband, Hugh, got an unexpected bonus at work. Miraculously, after tax and tithe, the bonus amount came to within $100 of the amount they had agreed to pay the nanny for the entire pregnancy! Jessica and Hugh knew at that moment that God really was taking care of them. This provision served as an amazing comfort to their family as they faced the long months of Jessica's bed rest ahead of them. "We knew that we could trust God no matter how hard our circumstances were," Jessica says, hugging three-year-old Lucy, who sits on her lap—the baby that awaited them at the end of that trial, yet another evidence of God's blessing and provision.

His Purpose

Sometimes it's hard to accept that God can bring about His purposes through our trials. It's hard to see past our circumstances to a future that, for us, doesn't exist yet. But God is not constrained by time. He is not reined in by our circumstances. Because of this, we have to trust that our limited perspective simply cannot process His higher purpose. We're often tempted during these times to wrestle back the control from Him, telling Him through our actions that He can't be trusted. We say to Him, "I got this one, God."

David writes of this tendency in Psalm 103:1–2: "Bless the LORD, O my soul, and all that is within me, bless his holy name. Bless the LORD, O my soul, and *do not forget all his benefits*" (NRSV, emphasis added). David knew he constantly needed to remind himself of what the Lord had done for him—and what He would do for him in the future. Like the rest of us, David struggled with remembering that God has a purpose in every trial, and a benefit waiting for those who will persevere.

This is especially true when we're in the continual process of surrendering our finances to Him. We tend to get worried and emotional, thinking He must not see the needs we're facing, and the impending devastation we feel is inevitable. However, the saying "God is rarely early but never late" most definitely applies in these situations. Our challenge—both physically and spiritually—is to wait. "Never run impulsively ahead of the Lord. Learn to await His timing—the second, minute and hour hand must all point to the precise moment for action."[2]

I remember a time I ran impulsively ahead of the Lord. We were in need of a computer and had a little money we could spend. In one of our "state of the union" meetings, we discussed whether a computer would be a wise use of this money. Since we were still in the stages of paying off debt, that money could have been earmarked toward one of our debts, so it was hard to spend it elsewhere. As I prayed about this decision, I felt God telling me to wait on this purchase. "God," I responded, "we can't wait any longer. We need a computer." I couldn't understand why He would tell me to wait, so I moved ahead with our plans to buy a computer. I didn't trust Him with my future and tried to solve a problem on my own. I had wrestled back the control once again.

About a month after we got this new computer, my mom called me to ask if we still needed a computer. "Well, no," I told her, "we bought one already. Why?" She went on to explain that her friends were getting rid of a nearly new computer because they'd decided to buy a laptop. Did we want it? In that moment I felt God whisper to me, "I told you to wait." Even though this was a difficult lesson to learn, it was a very powerful lesson that I have not forgotten. We ended up with two computers but minus a large chunk of money that could have gone to paying off debt. God used this lesson to teach me that I have to wait on His purpose to be accomplished. Beth Moore wrote, "We are wise to trust Him when He seems to be leading us contrary to those things we want to do or those things that seem to be so rational and fitting."[3] Even when I don't understand and even when it's hard to wait, waiting anyway is part of growing in faith as we simultaneously grow in our relationship with Him. As our dependence on Him grows, so does our relationship with Him. In this way, our financial journey becomes intertwined with our spiritual one.

His Peace

There will be times when an immediate resolution does not emerge—when we simply have to walk through what lies before us. We may find that God has something waiting for us on the other side of the experience, but we may have to wait until we get to heaven to know the reason. When these times come—when miraculous provisions and an ultimate purpose remain just out of our reach—our faith is stretched farther than we thought possible. We find the key to peace as we press into God, clinging to Him as we have never done before. My friend, author and speaker Mary DeMuth, shares a time like this in her family's life:

Our family of five had been missionaries in France for nearly five months when we got the call from our former mortgage lender. "You're late on your payments," they told us.

"Late? How can that be?" I asked. "We sold our house five months ago."

Thus began a long journey of pain and discovery. Turns out, we'd sold our home to a con man. We met him through a prayer meeting at church. His buying our home just as we left for France seemed like a godsend; instead it became a nightmare. Six months later we were forced to go through foreclosure. All our hard work at being debt free, managing our money wisely, and giving back to the Lord seemed to be a waste. In one instant, our stellar credit was destroyed. All this while we were serving God overseas.

During that time, my emotions roller-coastered between trusting God fully and worrying incessantly. But one day I woke up and felt peace. I realized either I believed God was our provider or I didn't. I let our house go. I let our credit score go. I let the betrayal and sadness go. I let the bewilderment and fear go. And I trusted God to take care of us.

No miracles happened. We still lost our home and our credit. But I wouldn't change the lesson I learned. To be peaceful when the world swirled around in confusion and unpredictability was a gift I'll cherish forever.

Four years later, we still suffer the consequences of the con man's actions.

And I'm often tempted to worry, get angry, and plunge into despair over the unfairness of it all. Thankfully, God keeps reminding me that He owns it all and He will provide in His way. I'm doing my best to rest there.

Mary's story is a wonderful reminder of God's continued care for us. Even when He chooses not to offer deliverance, He will still extend His hand and offer something that, in the end, is much richer—His perfect, abiding peace. John 14:27 puts it perfectly, "Peace I leave with you; my peace I give you. I do not give to you as the world gives. Do not let your hearts be troubled and do not be afraid."

Based on our experiences and the shared wisdom of others, the following few tips can help you prepare for unexpected expenses:

1. Surround yourself with a community of believers. Make investments in people whenever you can—not with the desire to get something out of it, but with the knowledge that all we send into other's lives comes back into our own. Over time, this will become a lifestyle for not only you, but your whole family.

2. Have a fund that you make deposits into regularly to help offset unexpected costs. This comes in handy when the dishwasher breaks, the car needs repairs, or an unexpected medical cost crops up. A fund like this will keep you from running to credit cards to bail yourself out.

3. Have a disaster plan. Spend some time strategizing how you would handle certain situations. Are there people you could go to for help? Holdings you would liquidate? Troubleshoot with your spouse, playing "what if." Though it might not be a pleasant conversation, it helps to be prepared—even if it's just emotionally.

4. Check on expiration dates and fine print details of insurance policies, warranties, deeds, and any legal documents or paperwork you may have. Know the details of your homeowner's insurance. What does it cover in case of fire or other disasters?

5. Place valuables and original copies in a safety deposit box.

6. Do background checks on those you allow to handle your money or are going to do business with—even if they profess to be Christians and seem "nice."

7. Draw up a will and carry enough life insurance for each spouse to live comfortably. (Rule of thumb is ten times your annual income.)

8. Check up on business or financial transactions even if they seem taken care of and don't just take the word of other people. If something seems fishy or "too good to be true" it just might be.

9. Remember that God is bigger than your circumstances no matter what happens.

■ STUDY

Read Deuteronomy 3:22; Psalm 50:9–12; Matthew 25:34–40; and Romans 12:4–8.

■ REFLECT, DISCUSS, PLAN

1. Are you plugged into a group of believers—through a church, a Bible study, or other community group? How are you investing in them and they in you?

2. Do you allow others to help you when difficult times come along?

3. Do you have stories of God's power, His provision, His people, His purpose, or His peace being brought into sharper focus through your financial journey? If so, share them with others. If you're going through this book in a group, consider sharing your story with the other members of the group as a testimony of God's goodness. If you're going through the book on your own, ask God to show you one person who needs to hear your story. Respond in obedience by making time to sit down and share what God has done in your life.

■ TAKE ACTION

Choose one of the tips to help you prepare for unexpected expenses and do it this week. Better yet, do it today!

Chapter 10

AVOIDING THE EASY BUTTON

Marybeth

When I found out that our second child was going to be a girl, I went a little crazy. I'd wanted a daughter for as long as I could remember, so her birth was the culmination of a lot of little-girl dreams. I set out to buy her the cutest outfits and the best, most beautiful nursery I could put together. The trouble was we didn't have any money. And my sweet husband—as wonderful a father as he is—failed to see the necessity of a cute nursery for a baby who would care very little about it. In hindsight, he was right, of course. But I couldn't see that at the time. I had tunnel vision. All I could see was pink and lace and all the frills. I was a woman on a mission and nothing could stop me, especially a little problem like money.

And so I did something terrible. I got a credit card that Curt knew nothing about. I put down all our financial information, signed the application, and sent it off. When the beautiful piece of plastic came in the mail with a $2000 limit on it, I was euphoric. I could create a beautiful nursery with $2000! The sad part is, I really thought I had come up with a creative solution to a problem my *husband* had. I was proud of myself. I spent freely, plunking down the credit card at stores around our city, justifying the purchases in my heart every step of the way. It wasn't for me, I told myself. It was for my daughter. I got things on sale, I reasoned. I was only doing what any good parent would do. And on and on it went.

But no matter how much I justified, I knew it was wrong to hide a credit card from my husband. I kept intercepting the bills my entire pregnancy, warding off the inevitable confrontation that would occur when he found out about my deceit. I'd covered my tracks pretty well, but I didn't anticipate him getting the bill while I was in the hospital after her birth. He showed up to visit with the bill in his hand. "Tell me there's another explanation for this," he said hopefully. I used my being in the hospital, recovering from childbirth to my full advantage—tears and all. To this day I'm just glad he found out when he did. He had an extra measure of compassion for me—which probably kept him from strangling me! We added that debt to the rest of the pile and went on. But our baby girl's nursery was never the source of joy I'd hoped for. When I looked at it I felt only guilt over what I'd done.

The Danger of *Deserve*

I'd fallen into the trap of uttering the most dangerous word in the world: *deserve*. I convinced myself that, in honor of the birth of my first daughter, I deserved to create a beautiful nursery for her. Furthermore, my daughter deserved to have a beautiful nursery. The child wasn't even born yet, and I was setting her up to believe in what she deserved! *Deserve*, I'm convinced, is the most dangerous word we can think or utter. It rots away our insides and makes us hard to live with. It motivates us to lie and cheat and steal to get what we want. It urges us in the wrong direction—far, far away from where God wants us to be. Satan whispers this dangerous word in our ears, turning our hearts inward.

I first became aware of how self-centered and ugly the word *deserve* really is when I heard it come from my teenage son's mouth. He'd get upset about something we'd denied him and spout off about how he deserved whatever it was. He deserved to have that outfit he wanted. He deserved money to spend at the mall even though he hadn't worked for it. He deserved his own room. He deserved a cell phone. And on and on and on it went. Listening to my son made me realize how I must sound to God at times.

Hollering about what we deserve hardly reflects the attitude His Word calls us to have. Micah 6:8 says, "He has showed you, O man, what is good. And what does the LORD require of you? To act justly and to love mercy and to walk humbly with your God." This verse says nothing about what we deserve. To be honest, all we really deserve is death. It's only through what Jesus did for us on the cross and God's grace and love that we have anything at all.

Financial Finagling

When we put our house on the market, we saw how easily a business transaction like selling a piece of property and purchasing another can become a decision based on emotion and impulse. Just recently, a young couple looked at our house but decided that, though they loved and wanted it, they needed to wait one more year before buying a house. I started thinking, *Wouldn't it be great to work something out with them.* A house that we'd looked at had just posted a "lease/purchase" sign, and I quickly schemed that we could let the young couple lease/purchase our home while we lease/purchased this other home. I presented the option to Curt, hoping he'd throw caution to the wind and say *yes*—even though I know him better than that.

Instead, he posed a couple of worst-case scenarios: What if they back out at the end of the year and don't go forward with the purchase? What if they move out in the middle of the year and we have to cover our mortgage and the lease price of the other home? And then he said something he's said to me many times: "When you start finagling the situation to make it work for you, you're venturing into dangerous territory that you're certain to regret later." I knew he was right and was grateful that he's able to be wise and rational when I'm emotional and impulsive. Deep down I know that finagling and manipulating is an easy-button solution. It's me trying to make something happen faster than it's supposed to so my agenda can be accomplished. I can be a slow learner in this area.

This false belief that we are owed something—that we deserve certain things in life—keeps us searching for the easy button. This concept has been popularized by a chain of office supplies, advertising that their products make running a business much simpler. Got a problem? Just press the easy button! This is not just an entertaining ad campaign, it's a way of life. "I want it all," the song by rock group Queen says, "and I want it now." Not only do we want material things, but we want to get them the easiest way possible. We deserve to open our hands and have blessings fall into them. This belief leads us to a path of shortcuts and quick fixes. When our money is at stake, though, this path is dangerous to take and easy to wander down.

Market Madness

Our friends Pete and Katherine decided that they were going to flip a house as a shortcut to wealth. This popular concept has been the subject of its own television show and numerous magazine and newspaper articles. The concept seems simple enough: buy a house in need of repair, fix it up, and resell it at a profit. Pete and Katherine knew a lot about fixing up houses through renovating their own home, so they decided to use their knowledge to make some quick money. There's nothing wrong with flipping houses, but there can be a huge financial risk in doing it. In hindsight, Pete and Katherine found several problems with their easy-button solution. After eighteen months of struggling with their decision, they've identified several problems that had been unforeseeable:

The project was too big. *We thought our estimate was enough to cover the cost of renovations, but we quickly found out we didn't have enough money to renovate to the degree we'd envisioned—including creating a second floor. We'd budgeted the project to the penny and to be completed over a certain amount of time, and everything exceeded our projections.* The project took too long. *The house we bought was in a historic district, and a historical district board controlled what we did. Waiting on approvals and scheduling our work around their meetings messed with us big time. This kink almost doubled the length of the project and increased construction costs by $70,000.*

We tried to sell in a poor market. *We learned you can't depend on the market to stay the same, and you never know when things are going to change. The market was booming when we started, but quickly turned—and now we can't sell the house. What was supposed to earn us some quick money became a millstone around our necks. It costs us $5,200 a month to carry the home every month we don't sell.*

Flipping houses isn't the only way that people's credit and finances can get ruined. Get-rich-quick and crazy financing schemes abound. Before making these kinds of decisions we need to take time to pray and seek God's will. Many times what He tells us to do will run contrary to what the world is telling us to do. In these moments we have a choice—we can pursue our own way, or His. Pursuing our own way will most always come back to haunt us.

Our friends Stephanie and Bryan were on top of the world and had a life others envied. They had a beautiful home in a gated community and enjoyed a solid financial foundation. But there was something else that tugged at them—a dream of living on some land where they could raise animals and give their four beautiful children room to run and explore.

One day they drove past their dream house and discovered it was for sale. They quickly bought the dream house and put the other house on the market, reasoning that it must be God's will that the new house was for sale and counting on Him to see that their other house sold quickly. They didn't spend a lot of time praying or seeking counsel. In hindsight, they say that they should have spent more time discerning God's will before buying the second house, trusting Him on the sale of their other home first and to preserve the dream home if it was His will for them to have it.

Two years later, as I write this, they still own both houses. The financial foundation they worked hard to create has been ruined. Their easy button—buying one house through a bridge loan so they didn't lose it to other buyers—didn't work out the way they thought it would. They took a risk, and they lost. They've lived through two years of two mortgage payments, two electric bills, two water bills, and taxes on two properties. The savings they'd built up is gone, and they've taken on tens of thousands in credit card debt just to survive.

This trial has affected every area of their lives. What was once a picture of security and careful planning is now a picture of devastation and hopelessness. Stephanie and Bryan gave me permission to share this story with you in hopes that perhaps another couple would not be tempted to press the easy button as a way to fast-track the good life.

The good news is, Stephanie and Bryan's story doesn't end there—and neither does any of ours. Even when we make foolish financial decisions, God is there to help us and to offer His hand. Though we may not have sought Him initially, He has not abandoned us. We have the hope of a future that looks different than where we are now. It might not be an easy road to get there, and it might look like a lot of work from where we're standing, but there's a way out. And sometimes, we find that even the way is part of God's miraculous plan for us. Working all things together for good (Rom. 8:28) in the most unexpected way is God's specialty.

The Faithfulness of God

Pete and Katherine have certainly found this to be true. While the financial burden of carrying their flip house has caused them to struggle far more than they ever anticipated, it's also brought about unforeseen blessings they couldn't have otherwise found. Pete gave me permission to reprint a letter here that he sent out to their close friends and family. I think this letter shows what God did during this difficult time, and how He was never far away. Even at their lowest points, they found Him faithful.

While a lot of bad things happened to us, some awesome things happened as well. I know that some of you don't believe that God works in people's lives or that He cares about house flipping projects, but bear with me while I share some miracles that occurred in our lives during this time:

Miracle #1. *When the house wasn't selling, we were faced with having to drop the price, which we did. When I got down to our break-even point I was very reluctant (to understate the matter) to drop the price. We decided that $20,000 was the amount, but we still couldn't bring ourselves to do it. I had to face the horrible truth that instead of earning money from this house, once we dropped the price, we were going to have to pay money to sell the house. To me, this was the ultimate point of admitting defeat. The very day I bit the bullet and dropped the price, I was called into my boss's office and notified that I had received a "Key Contributor" award for my performance at work. It was for exactly $20,000.*

Miracle #2. *We had stopped giving money to our church because we needed every bit of money we had just to feed our family. Both of us knew that wasn't the right answer, but it made sense on paper. God doesn't need the money, we rationalized, but we do. Well, one day out of the blue one of my coworkers who knew the house situation (but not that we had stopped giving) randomly asked me, "Do you know the reason why we give?" This question hit me hard, and God used it to speak to me. That Sunday, with much hesitation, we finally dropped a check in. It was like falling backward and hoping that someone would catch us. Well, we got home from church and not even two hours later a person stopped by my house that I had not seen in a year and a half. He handed me a check for $250. I said, "What's this for?"*

He said, "I'm paying you back." He explained that we had given him money at a time of need a long time ago. I insisted that it was a gift, but he insisted that I take it. I accepted, knowing that God was giving me money for food that month and showing that He would provide. This was a valuable lesson about continuing to give even in the midst of what we were going through.

Miracle #3. *We went up to my mom's river house for Christmas. We didn't buy much in the way of gifts because we couldn't. We openly regifted things from our home and got one or two small things for the kids. We all talked about this as a family, and everyone knew it would be light on the gifts. Yet, instead of that Christmas being a sad time, we had a great Christmas with our extended family. After a great trip we drove back, the weight of our situation weighing heavier and heavier as we got closer and closer to home. We had an extra house, no lookers, no food, and lots of creditors waiting for us. About a week after we got back I got a call completely out of the blue from a business partner that I had not talked to in over a year. We had dissolved our business, and I fully expected that I would never hear from him again.*

He was calling to ask if I was interested in a consulting job. I said "yes." I was just hoping for enough money to pay all our bills in January. What happened still blows my mind. The contract he sent me states that I will help his company by answering questions between 6 to 9 PM, Monday through Friday, a job that I can do in addition to my regular job. I am retained for three months for $4,000 per month whether or not they call me. I have had 5 to 6 one-hour calls to date. To top it all off, because it is a travel company, they are throwing in a Caribbean cruise if I simply make myself available for the length of the contract. They have paid faithfully, which has allowed us to carry the house for almost three months while we ride out this bad market. God has also provided some other contract work that will net us back the $50,000 we stand to lose when the house sells. These jobs came out of the blue, falling into my lap with no warning. I know without a doubt this is not me, but is simply God working in our lives. If it was just one of these things, then I might agree with you that it was just a coincidence. But it is a series of "Godincidences," to borrow a term from my mom.

You might ask yourself like we did, why does God care about us flipping a house and if we make money or not? Why would He do these things? We don't deserve this. We made the bad decisions to get us here. The answer we have gotten very clearly is that it is not about the house or the money. This whole thing has been about faith, and God building our character. He has not left us in financial ruin or even without food and a roof over our heads.

While we are still in the midst of this, I am confident that we will be okay. God has done great things, and He won't leave us hanging now. Though we still can't sell it, we have been able to rent the house, which has helped us with the month-to-month costs a lot. While it doesn't cover the entire amount, we are able to breathe easier.

There is more I could tell you about the neighbor who is out to make things difficult for us and ended up costing us a lot of money and time. I could tell you about the injustices that occurred in the many meetings we had with the historical district board and how their own lawyer said we have a case to sue them. I could tell you about the hundreds of calls we got from creditors and how Katherine and I could have had enough reason to divorce three times over. But that is not what is so unique about this. It is what God did to protect us even during all of that.

Here are some of the other things that I thank God for:

- *Our kids know what it is like to scrape together meals from Hamburger Helper and Ramen noodles multiple times a week.*
- *They know what it is like not to get Christmas or birthday gifts from their parents. And not to get an allowance or get paid for extra work around the house.*
- *They know what it is like to sacrifice personally, doing hard manual labor at the flip house for no pay because we couldn't pay to have work done.*
- *They know what it is like not to be able to go to the movies with friends, get new clothes or shoes, play sports, or go out to dinner for months at a time.*
- *After seeing us go through the problems with the historic district board and the neighbor who decided to make our lives miserable, our kids know what it means not to get bitter or angry when they are faced with people who intentionally cause harm or when there is a grave injustice against them. They have witnessed God's peace reigning in our lives and seen us treat*

these people as Jesus would have—even when we didn't
want to.

‣ *One of my favorite things is that, out of necessity,*
Katherine started to cook dinner at home again. We
have dinner together almost every night and talk and
laugh and hang around even after eating some nights.
We never used to do that, and it is a gift that has come
from this time. I treasure these memories around our
table, which is something we never would have done
otherwise.

Pete's letter is an example of God at work even in the toughest of circumstances. God knows that sometimes He has to bring us out to bring us in. Deuteronomy 6:23 says, "But he brought us out from there to bring us in and give us the land that he promised on oath to our forefathers." He has to take us out of an old lifestyle, an old sense of entitlement, an old view of what we deserve. By taking us out of that, He can lead us into a life that is surrendered to Him. In doing so we lay claim to our own promised land. A land that is not accessible via an easy button, but a place you value all the more because of the struggle you endured to find it.

■ STUDY

Read Psalm 15; Proverbs 30:7–9; and 1 Timothy 6:6–10, 17–21.

■ REFLECT, DISCUSS, PLAN

1. Do you have a story about when you have pressed the easy button? Has this chapter brought back memories of how that worked out for you?
2. Perhaps you're considering an easy-button solution. Has this chapter caused you to reconsider this option? Is God asking you instead to walk through a solution that might take a bit longer,

but will offer more security and will honor Him with your obedience and trust?

3. What has God brought you out of to bring you into? If you
are in the midst of that journey right now, praise Him that He
knows where He is leading you. Rejoice that He has the destination under control and that you can trust Him to get you there.

■ TAKE ACTION

Spend some time praying—preferably together—for wisdom in your
decisions. Ask God to hem you in from taking the easy-button routes
that might only land you in bigger trouble.

Chapter 11

EXPERIENCING THE BLESSINGS OF FINANCIAL HARDSHIP

Marybeth

The phone rang, the sound like sandpaper against my frayed nerves. Every day was a new day of facing challenges, never knowing where our next obstacle would crop up. Perhaps it would be a new set of expenses we hadn't anticipated, or a new bill showing up in the mailbox that would be added to the growing pile that could not be paid. The day would most certainly include calls from creditors and collections agents. That I could count on. In the days before caller ID, we had no way to tell who was calling, so there was no way to screen our calls. I handled it by simply not answering my calls. My closest friends knew why I didn't answer and shook their heads in disbelief at what we were facing.

For some reason on this day—though I knew it was probably a collector calling to demand I pay my bill—I answered the phone. I felt strong and hopeful as I answered the call. I hoped that it was a friend calling to say "hi" and offer encouragement. Instead, the caller asked for me in that stilted, formal voice I'd learned to recognize as a collector. They'd usually ask for "the Wall-ens," instead of the Way-lens. I braced myself internally, but nothing could have prepared me for this guy.

I was used to offering excuses and making empty promises, then hanging up with that familiar knot in my stomach, any scrap of joy I'd been holding onto being disconnected along with the phone call. But I was not familiar with this man's tactics. He was abusive. He was abrasive. He was menacing. He all but threatened to come and get my firstborn child while I slept if I didn't make some sort of arrangement right then and there. In the midst of all of this, Curt walked in from work and took the phone, only to be berated as well. I don't remember exactly how we left it with this person, but I do know that Curt ended the call by telling him not ever to call our house again and never to speak to his wife that way again. I was near tears as I looked at Curt for assurance. "Can he really do all those things he was saying?" I asked him, fear etched on my face. He shook his head, visibly shaken.

"I'm not sure what he can do, but I know I won't take any more of that kind of abuse from any creditor," he said. "I know that I'm doing the very best I can. And that's all I can do." We went through the motions of dinner and bedtime with the kids, but our minds were still on that phone call, our spirits doused by this man's behavior. I don't know that we ever felt as hopeless as we did that night.

Even now, ten years later, I wonder about that man and how he sleeps at night. I know that our name was only one on a long list of calls he would place in a single evening, venting his own anger on these unsuspecting people. If you had told me that night that some day I'd be writing about the blessings of financial hardship, I would have most certainly told you that you were crazy. I would have never believed that I could find blessings in the midst of all that we were facing.

But I did.

As I reflect on that night, I feel sorry for those two young people who truly were doing the very best they could. A string of bad financial decisions, coupled with a monumental medical emergency, had left them crippled but not paralyzed, broken but not beyond repair, down but not out. And that is the happy news in our sad little story—that

God can rebuild anything, even if it means starting from the ground up. The same resurrection power that raised Jesus from the dead is still at work in our lives. If He can bring the dead to life, then He can certainly breathe new life into your finances. We wouldn't know that truth in the deepest parts of our hearts had it not been for the financial issues we lived through. And live through them we did. Though at times, in all honesty, it seemed like we would not. Proverbs 13:12 says, "Hope deferred makes the heart sick." And we can both testify that this is so true. We remember being so heartsick over our finances that we felt like we'd literally die. And yet, as we look back on that time, we see that God was always faithful to send hope just when we needed it most.

Curt

It's hard to describe the range of emotions that I experienced when we were deeply in debt. It's hard to explain the depth of the feelings of despair and hopelessness. After our son had spent months in the hospital going through many procedures, our medical bills had gotten outrageous. Even with a good insurance plan, the deductibles and co-pays were in the thousands of dollars. Our normal bills were months behind, we were deeply in debt with credit cards, student loans, and the IRS, and now we were getting medical collection agencies calling our home. I lost the ability to function. Marybeth was living at the hospital with our youngest son, and I could barely get our oldest two kids to where they were going for the day. I would arrive at work and literally stare at my computer screen for hours at a time, trying to manage the paralyzing fear that consumed my thoughts. I knew it was only a matter of time before we lost everything.

An Unexpected Answer to Prayer

One evening when I arrived home from work and started going through the mail, I opened a letter from the hospital where our son was being treated. The letter stated that unless I paid a bill that totaled $2,400 within ten days, the hospital was going to take me to court. I've learned more about the collection process and, looking back, realize that the letter was probably just a scare tactic. But for a young husband and father, that letter seemed to symbolize what a failure my life had become. Finding that kind of money was impossible. I had a mountain of debt with no way to make the payments. Our situation was hopeless, and I carried that lack of hope deep within my soul.

A few days later, in the middle of the workday, I did something that I'd never done before. I got up from my desk, drove home to our empty house, walked in, and literally fell face down before God. I couldn't hold back the sobs as months and months of pressure burst through my tough, prideful exterior. My prayer was simple and my words were few: "I don't know what to do . . . please help me . . ."

I'm not sure how long I stayed like that, but I eventually realized that it was time for me to go pick up my two oldest kids. Ten years later, the only thing that I remember feeling as I left our home was emptiness.

Life went on as usual for a few days. But then I got the phone call. My grandmother called our home to let me know that her brother in Erie, Pennsylvania, had just sold the home he'd been living in for the past forty years, and he wanted her to pass along a message. Although he didn't know what our exact needs might be, he was aware that our son had been undergoing a lot of medical treatments since his birth. Uncle CG wanted to help our family financially.

His message—what he wanted her to pass along—was that a few days ago he had put a check in the mail for $2,400. My grandmother had gotten it and wanted me to come by her house to get it.

When I hung up the phone, I was crying again, but for a completely different reason. I realized, maybe for the very first time in my life, that my Father in heaven really did care about me. Those things that I had read in the Bible became much more than words. His love became real. He had His arms around me and was watching over everything that was going on. I felt a spark of *hope* begin to burn inside my heart.

I realized that I wasn't facing these problems alone. My Father was fighting alongside of me: "We are hard pressed on every side, but not crushed; perplexed, but not in despair; persecuted, but not abandoned; struck down, but not destroyed" (2 Cor. 4:8–9).

Marybeth

I love that story! It's become one of the top ten "God moments" in our family's history. But the story doesn't end there. During that same time, as we were reeling from all of Matthew's medical bills and needs, my Christian Mother's Group held their annual Christmas gift raffle. This was always a highlight of everyone's year, as we all brought something to donate, then bought raffle tickets to bid on the items. Typically we'd donate the money we raised from the sale of the tickets to some charity. When my mom said she wanted to go, I didn't think a thing of it, as I knew she'd enjoy it. I never suspected that she had another motive for being there. I walked around like everyone else, having fun and trying for a brief time to focus on Christmas and not my own personal issues.

After the raffle was over and all the prizes had been distributed, Margie Eades, the leader of this special group, called me to the front and presented me with the check for all the proceeds for that day. My mom was crying and so were many of my friends. I was in shock. How did they know? How would they *ever* know how much that gift meant? With their money we were able to buy a few gifts for our children's Christmas and pay an urgent medical bill we'd just been discussing. That morning we had no idea how we'd pay it. And then, through God's people and His favor, we had our answer.

An Unlikely Place to Bloom

A few weeks ago, I noticed my pot of summer flowers had fallen victim to the frost, a foretaste of winter. The stalks of what had once been vibrantly colored blooms lay shriveled and lifeless. I instantly missed the flowers that had made my time in the laundry room just a bit more bright and beautiful. With eight people in our house, I spend quite a bit of time in the laundry room, as you can imagine. Every time I glanced out my laundry room window, those flowers had brightened my day. Although I was sorry they were gone, I took comfort in the seeds lying dormant under the soil that would return again next summer. Everyone needs something to look forward to.

Today, after a burst of unseasonably warm temperatures, I noticed one lone flower had popped up unexpectedly. How brilliant its colors stood in stark contrast to the dead brown plants that lay beside it. How silly this little flower seemed, waving to me as though it were the middle of summer, unaware that it was not its time to bloom. The little flower seemed strangely confident that, despite its surroundings and circumstances, it was meant to bloom for such a time as this. As I pondered where this little flower had come from, I felt my heavenly Father gently remind me that I am a lot like that flower. I have managed to bloom in the most unlikely of places.

Unless you've lived this life of truly walking in faith and belief in God's provision, you can't get to the place of living a life of faith on a whole new level. My friend Lysa TerKeurst, author of *What Happens When Women Say Yes to God*, says, "How can I claim to be a woman of faith if I live a life that requires very little faith?" That has certainly been true in our faith walk of trusting God to restore and redeem our finances. Though we've certainly made our share of mistakes and unwise decisions, God has always lovingly and gracefully showed us compassion and given us a way out. While the path hasn't always been straightforward and as direct as we'd like, we've seen that the path was taking us exactly where we needed to go. Even to a place of writing this book and sharing this story.

God's lessons for us did not end with miraculous provisions. We've also seen Him growing our characters and strengthening our marriage. Through our time of struggling with finances, we've been forced to make changes in our lifestyle. We think things through, and weigh whether purchases are really necessary. We've learned to be self-disciplined and less impulsive in our spending habits. We're more intentional in every aspect of our expenditures—from gas to groceries. We think about where every dollar goes. I dare say that this process has made us better individuals.

We've made it our mission to make getting out of debt—and changing the habits that got us there—a priority. This united purpose has ultimately unified us instead of dividing us as it once threatened to do. When we first got married, as we've said, we never talked about money—unless we were fighting about it. Money was nothing but a source of contention between us. We were both angry about the state of our finances, yet for a long time felt powerless to do anything about it. Over time, this combined feeling of anger and powerlessness can destroy a marriage if allowed to fester and reproduce. We had to learn to communicate about the feelings that led to the anger long before those feelings led to strife. We've learned to lay down our own wants and desires and give sacrificially to our children and to each other. And we've experienced the deep, abiding blessings that flow from living a life of sacrifice. I believe that this lesson has made us more giving on many levels, and has changed our hearts for the better—including turning them to each other.

My friend Stephanie, whose story of carrying two mortgages for over two years was told in the previous chapter, told me that, while she would never have chosen to go through their difficulties, she wouldn't trade the experience. For the first time in her life she's learned what it means to be truly dependent on God, and has been forced to slay her pride like never before. She said that walking through this time has been a unique cycle of depending on God, experiencing His miraculous provision, trusting Him more as a result of the provision, and finding herself wanting to obey Him in every other area of her life as a result. As she and her family have walked through this time, they have been painfully stretched yet lovingly comforted. "Had God 'rescued' us out of the situation a year ago," she told me, "we would never have learned these lessons. We would never have grown in our faith as we have through this. I can't tell you the number of times He has miraculously provided for us. It would take a whole book! He has used this financial crisis to make us into totally different people. People I like a whole lot more than the people we used to be."

Stephanie's words ring true for Curt and me as well. We've felt those same feelings and experienced that strange paradox of being grateful for a trial we never would have chosen. These are lessons that will stay with us for the rest of our lives.

As of this writing we've at last achieved being completely debt free. Not only are we filled with praise for God, we're certain that we never want to go back to being slaves to debt. In the meantime, as we struggled to reach this place, we sought God in every decision, we placed our trust in Him, we honored Him with our money, and we thanked Him for every opportunity He allowed to stretch us, to grow us, and to conform us to His image. What started as a daily lesson has turned into a way of life. We learned firsthand that there are indeed blessings to be found along the way, if only we will look for them.

> Jesus replied, "You do not realize now what I am doing, but later you will understand." (John 13:7)

■ STUDY

In this chapter, we shared some of our personal memories of God's goodness and miraculous provision. We also testified to how God has changed us from the inside out. If we hadn't written about and captured these circumstances and challenges as they happened, we would likely forget the lessons God had for us. Read the following verses: Psalm 25:4–7; Proverbs 7:1–3; Malachi 3:16; and 1 Corinthians 10:11–12.

■ REFLECT, DISCUSS, PLAN

1. Why do you think remembering what God has done is important in the area of finances?
2. How do you and your spouse react when things go wrong

financially? Do you separate and internalize what's going on, or band together and cry out to God?

3. Have you acknowledged God and trusted Him fully with your finances? Have you seen His hand at work in your lives as a result?

■ TAKE ACTION

Begin a journal chronicling your financial journey. Write down your current debt and any amounts you've paid off. Note any debt you pay off from now on. Write down any personal examples of God's provision and lessons He has taught you through this journey. Once you begin this journey, stay committed to documenting not what you've done in your own strength but what God has done for you and what He has delivered you from. Use this journal in your prayer time as you offer up praises to Him and give Him the glory, and share these examples and lessons with anyone God places in your life who desperately needs to hear your story of hope.

Always be prepared to give an answer to everyone who asks you to give the reason for the hope that you have. (1 Peter 3:15)

Chapter 12

REPLACING COMPARISON WITH CONTENTMENT

Marybeth

There's a sign in our yard: "For Sale." This move has been a long time in coming as we lived in a house that was decidedly smaller than the homes of our friends. Though we were committed not to move until we had our debt paid off, sticking to it was hard at times. As we watched all our friends buy homes with nearly double the square footage and about half the kids, we looked around us and fell victim to wondering why we couldn't have more. It was hard when our children wanted to know why so-and-so had a big playroom or so-and-so didn't have to share a bedroom. As the older ones became teens, the issues got more serious as they vented their frustration with our situation. We had to remind them that we were blessed to have a roof over our heads and use those moments as a reminder to them of the dangers of debt. "Ultimately," we told them, "you have to pay the piper." And that's what we've spent years doing—reaping the consequences of frivolous spending and unwise financial decisions. We hope our honesty with them will ward off their own bad financial choices in adulthood.

During the time that we lived in our small(er) home, it didn't help me when my friends—good, Christian friends—made little remarks like, "I don't know how you all live in that tiny house!" Though they were just kidding, and at times even trying to compliment me for my fortitude, their words still stung. I knew I had less than they had. I'd been to their large homes and seen their beautiful decor. Living with comments like that can stir up emotional conflict and cause a person who is struggling with spending to lapse into old habits if that person is in a weak place.

I've heard it said that comparison is the death of contentment. This is so true. You might be fine and dandy, enjoying your life and appreciating your blessings until your friend gets something better, nicer, or bigger than you. Then suddenly you look at your life and it just doesn't measure up. What was fine before is now lacking in your eyes. This is also a reason I rarely go out and shop. I've learned that going to a mall and just wandering around looking at items is truly a dangerous activity. Doing it exposed me to wants I didn't even know I had. It's like an alcoholic going into a bar. The temptation is best avoided altogether. I shop now only when I have specific needs and the money in hand. I no longer carry credit cards so I'm not tempted to use them. I can't tell you how many times I used our "emergency cards" on a sale item and justified that as an emergency! If you're trying to get out of debt and change your spending habits, avoiding shopping as a recreational activity is a great place to start.

But avoiding the malls isn't a cure-all for comparison. The root of this problem goes much deeper than compulsive shopping. It goes to the very heart of what you believe about yourself and how you perceive that others see you. For many of us, comparison is a lifelong habit grounded in inferiority and based on a need for approval. This constant comparing leads to feelings of self-doubt and a diminished identity. The urge to compensate for these inadequate feelings drives us to do whatever it takes to raise our status in the eyes of others. This was certainly true of Curt and me in the early days of our marriage.

Curt

I've compared myself to others most of my life. As early as my young teenage years, I've been overly concerned with the clothes I wore, the car I drove, and the things I had. I didn't recognize it at the time, but I was deeply insecure and needed the affirmation of others. Most of the money I earned was used to buy things to make myself feel better. I loved music and always had the best stereo systems, Walkmans, and all the albums (yes, albums) of my favorite bands. Clothes were important to me, and I always bought the best brands from my favorite stores. In order to impress and keep up with my friends, I spent all I had, never putting any money aside for savings.

With such a poor understanding of how money should be managed, I was primed to make bad decisions when I had the opportunity to use debt to get what I wanted. This financial discontent followed me into my marriage. Marybeth and I wanted to achieve in just a few short years what took our parents a lifetime to build. I wanted to impress others, and rushed off to buy a new car. Everyone said that home ownership was a sign that you were financially successful, so Marybeth and I rushed into buying a new house years before we were ready. Then we used debt to get the furniture we "needed" to make our house look nice. Unfortunately, nothing we had was ever good enough. There was always a friend who had just a little bigger house or nicer car. For years, I compared myself to the wealth around me and told myself that I didn't measure up.

One of the biggest lessons I've learned over the past ten years is that being content has nothing to do with the way that others perceive you. True contentment has nothing to do with the location or size of my house, the age of my car, or the number of clothes in my closet. I've learned that the stuff I thought would make me happy has just been a shackle. I've lived most of my life miserable, trying to pay the bills that always come due. True contentment is being freed from the pressures of debt so that I can focus my life on things that matter most—my relationship with God and with my family.

Marybeth

A life invested in appearances and possessions is an empty life. Anyone who has chased that dream knows that it's nothing more than a mirage. It's like pushing a revolving door but never finding the entrance. Our desire to look good to others had consumed us and made us fools. Don't believe it? Here's an example: one time we decided we were going to decorate our guest bathroom in a popular golf theme. (Does anyone else remember this fad?) In order to get all the right accessories for our bathroom, we went to a local department store and bought a whole set of golf-motif items. One of those items was a decorative trashcan. I never even checked the price tags as we happily paid for our purchases with a swipe of the credit card. Later I saw the sticker on the bottom of the trashcan as I put it in the bathroom. I'd just bought a $25 trashcan! On credit! I still have that trashcan in my son's room with the price tag still affixed as a reminder of how foolish I once was.

We had certainly bought into the "never enough" mentality that pervades our culture. We were looking for happiness in all the wrong places, accepting the world's solutions to a spiritual condition. Those price tags added up over time—amounting to the crushing debt we eventually got tough enough to tackle. We were drowning in debt because we'd bought a lie. I could almost hear Satan laughing at his own joke. "Ha!" he would cackle in his evil hiss. "They bought it!" And bought it, we had. Literally.

Looking Good Versus Living Good

In the end, we had to make a choice. Though lots of emotions might cloud our ability to see this choice, it's really quite simple. We learned that we could either look good or live good. We had spent the first half of our marriage trying to look good. And it had nearly wrecked us. We decided to make whatever changes were necessary to start living good. Our first challenge was to adjust our perspective away from what others thought of us—or what we perceived they thought of us—and start focusing on what God thought of us.

As we dug deeper into God's opinion of us, we also discovered that His opinion about money and materialism is, like everything else, counter to the culture. We'd chased after the almighty dollar long enough. Having things, attaining positions, and pursuing wealth is not what God has designed us to pursue. Our hearts are prewired to long for Him and Him alone (Eccl. 3:11). Everything else is meaningless (Eccl. 2:11). If we follow Him and seek His design for abundant life (John 10:10), we will find what we desire in the depths of our souls. What was lost will be found—not in money or fashion or homes or cars—but in Him. We had to start living good.

There's an interesting thing about making this switch—when you stop striving to look good and start resting in living good, other people want what *you* have. They see the difference in you—the peace that passes all understanding. They're likely to make comments about the change in you or tell you that you're different from other people they know. They might even want to know why, which opens the door for you to share the reason. For so long both Curt and I wanted to be respected and admired for all the wrong reasons. We wanted our names to be famous. When we started living for God and stopped living for ourselves, we became consumed with making His name famous—sharing what He has done for us as a way to bring glory to His name, not ours. We understood for the first time that we are but dust (Ps. 103:14). We have nothing to offer apart from Him (John 15:5). The funny thing is, as soon as that became our focus, He began to add to our lives in surprising ways. We were living out Matthew 6:33: "But seek first his kingdom and his righteousness; and all these things will be given to you as well." For a long time we lived opposite of that; we wanted all these things without bothering to seek Him first.

> Give careful thought to your ways. You have planted much, but have harvested little. You eat, but never have enough. You drink, but never have your fill. You put on clothes, but are not

warm. You earn wages, only to put them in a purse with holes in it. (Hag. 1:5–6)

The key to living good is reflected in the first sentence of this verse. Giving careful thought to your ways means not spending haphazardly, with no regard for where the money is going or why. It means finding out what God wants us to do with our money. It means identifying what His desire for our lives really is. As we uncover the truth He has for us, we see that His plan has nothing to do with material things. Grasping this goes a long way toward dispensing with comparison, and instead discovering contentment. We had to learn where true joy and peace can be found, and embrace what it really means to store up treasure in heaven and not on earth (Matt. 6:19–21). We had to stop putting our money in purses with holes—moving from a mind-set of "never enough" and turning to the God who is enough. In this way, your financial journey becomes as much a spiritual journey as an economic one.

Finding Happiness

At some point in this process, I discovered a valuable question to ask myself: "But will it make me happy?" This was driven home to me when our son Bradley, who was about three at the time, went through a stage where he'd bat his eyes at me whenever I told him "no" and say, "But Mommy, it will make me happy." He'd do this when he wanted to stay up late when he really needed to go to bed, or when he wanted sweets before his nutritious dinner. He saw the immediate gratification of getting what he wanted; I saw the big picture of what he really needed. He was convinced that my goal as a mom should have been to indulge his every want. Instead of governing his choices to shape his character and help him grow up, he wanted his flesh to be satisfied. One day as I was thinking about his motives and chuckling over how cute he was when he said it, I realized how often I do this very same thing with my heavenly Father. "But God," I tell Him in my prayers, "it will make me happy." I get such tunnel vision about what I want that I don't see what's truly best for me. I'm not that different, I realized, from that three-year-old boy.

How many times in your life have you wanted something so badly—yet when you got whatever it was, you realized, "Nope, this didn't do it for me either." That house you wanted to move into, that person you wanted to date, that achievement you thought would bring success, that child you longed to have—they all brought you momentary happiness, but they didn't fulfill you as you'd hoped or bring you the significance you longed for. I'm learning slowly that whenever I find myself begging God for something, with some whining thrown in for good measure, I have to step back and ask myself the question, *But will it make me happy?* I know that whatever "it" is, it doesn't have the power to bring me lasting happiness—that deep indwelling joy that only God can bring. I may have a flash of happiness, only to lose it mere moments later. I'm learning slowly to push aside these momentary longings and seek God instead. To tell Him, "Here's what I think I want. But I trust You to do what's best for me."

I've learned that an outfit hanging in my closet that looks great on me, an accolade for my child, a trip to the spa, a book with my name on the cover, or an address in the right neighborhood will not make me happy, as much as I think it might. I can't look for happiness in the things of this earth, or I will certainly live in a state of disappointment. Instead, I can spend my time seeking God, and allowing Him to bring along unexpected blessings—little bouquets of happiness along the way. That doesn't mean I don't still look longingly at a new iPod or a sleek new laptop and think fleetingly, "Ooh, now that would make me happy." But I'm learning to pull back and refocus my perspective when I have those thoughts. Will it make me happy? Maybe for a moment. But in the long run, only God can bring me the joy I seek. I'm finding contentment in Him, minute by minute, day by day.

Turn your eyes upon Jesus,
Look full in his wonderful face,

And the things of earth will grow strangely dim,
In the light of his glory and grace.[1]

■ STUDY

Read Psalm 16:11; Galatians 6:2–5; Philippians 4:11–13; and Hebrews 13:5–6.

■ REFLECT, DISCUSS, PLAN

1. Do you know anyone who doesn't struggle with comparison and contentment? What do you see in them that has set them free from this struggle?
2. What do you see as key to being freed from comparison? Would this freedom lead you into a place of contentment? ·
3. Are you looking good or living good? What changes do you need to make in your life or attitudes to stop looking good and start living good?
4. How has comparison and contentment landed you in financial trouble in your past? If you're working through this book in a group, share a story with the group if you feel comfortable doing so. (Just think of my $25 trash can!)

■ TAKE ACTION

Are you modeling contentment to your spouse and children? Your friends, neighbors, and coworkers? The next time you're tempted to complain, consciously change gears and share a blessing in your life instead.

Chapter 13

BUILDING A
FINANCIAL LEGACY

Marybeth

Every year around Christmas, we enter a season I like to call "The Catalogs Are Coming! The Catalogs Are Coming!" Suddenly we receive a deluge of mail-order kid-friendly catalogs—and our kids are subjected to a daily parade of clothes, toys, games, and gadgets they didn't even know they wanted . . . until, of course, they saw the catalogs. These catalogs have the same effect on my children as a trip to the mall has on me. Suddenly they get a case of extreme gimmies. Our conversations are laced with lists of desires and wants. I cringe every time I see them coming, knowing they'll likely ask me for yet another item to add to their growing lists. It's exhausting.

Like me, you may have grown up hearing sayings like, "Money doesn't grow on trees." "Save for a rainy day." "Waste not, want not." But to me they were just sayings that didn't really mean anything. As we grew older we heard even more sayings. We heard, "Buy now, pay later." "Ninety days same as cash." "No interest until you're too old to care anymore." And that all sounded pretty good. With no one to step in and tell us any different, we believed what we were hearing. As we looked around, it seemed that everyone else was doing it, so why shouldn't we?

We wanted a different outcome for our children. We wanted their lives to be different from those of most people in the prevailing culture. We had to get intentional about shaping their legacy, and start at an early age.

The older kids get, the more aware they become of what's out there. Kids are not immune to materialism any more than we are, and retailers know that. What's more, retailers capitalize on it. Companies like Visa are vying to be the emblem on the fake credit cards included in children's toy cash registers. The two-trillion-dollar consumer credit card industry targets young people with credit card offers that entice them to take on debt at younger and younger ages. Author Mary Hunt says, "When attitudes of entitlement, financial ignorance and availability of easy credit occur at the same time within the heart of a child, they create a kind of 'perfect storm' that has all the likelihood of creating a disastrous situation."[1] How can we, as parents, combat that and lay a foundation of solid financial principles, helping our kids to rise above the trappings of a consumer driven culture? How can we change our children's financial future, helping them avoid the traps we ourselves may have fallen into? Here are seven points for parents to ponder:

1. *Debt is not normal or healthy.* The culture will tell your kids otherwise, so you must counter it at home. Let your kids see you save for things you want instead of financing them. Explain why you turned down that store credit card the clerk offered you when you checked out—even though it sounded like it would save you money. Explain what interest is, and show them how much you've paid in interest when you've bought things on credit. Put it in terms of things you could have bought for them with that money. Be honest about your mistakes and poor decisions with money in the past—especially in the area of taking on debt. Detail to them how much work it's taking you to get out of debt and the things you could be doing right now if you weren't paying off debt. Basically they should hate debt like they hate sin!

2. *Giving money to church is essential.* We tell our kids, "God honors those who honor Him." While I'm not preaching a prosperity doctrine here, I do believe that kids from an early age need to understand the importance of giving a portion of their money to their church. The earlier a habit is started, the more natural it becomes. Anytime our children get money from a grandparent, a job, or from us, we require them to immediately take ten percent out for church, twenty percent for savings, and the rest is theirs to keep. This process, then, becomes a mind-set. But believe me, at times they don't exactly like being required to do it—especially when they're saving for something and want to use all their money to buy it. We assure them that God will reward their commitment, and there have been many times they've seen God do so.

3. *Delayed gratification builds character.* You do your children a disservice if you don't teach them to wait. Better to learn this in the protection and nurture of your home than out in the world as adults. Purchasing something that's been anticipated and savored is a shining, memorable moment in a child's life—with much more value attached to that item in the end, I can assure you! The next time your children tell you they want something *now*, ask them how much money they have, and help them ponder how much they'll need to save. Help them think of some extra chores they can do to raise the money, then give them a goal to work toward, and help them plan how to reach their goal. They'll either forget about the item—showing you it would have been a waste of your hard-earned money—or embark on a character-building experience. While it might take a bit more time on your part, the lessons they learn will serve them the rest of their lives.

4. *Eating out and other forms of entertainment—like movies—are special treats, not a lifestyle.* Through Curt's financial counseling with numerous families, he's determined that a number-one budget buster for families is eating out and entertainment. We as parents

have learned to reward ourselves in that way, reasoning that we "deserve" it. (There's that word again!) Our children have been raised this way and have picked up on this mind-set. A shift in perspective for the entire family can save money and provide a more realistic attitude. Examine your family's attitude and budget in this area, and see if there are changes you need to make. Make going out to eat a treat instead of the norm, rent movies (they come out so soon now after release you hardly have to wait anymore!), and have a family movie night complete with popcorn and sleeping bags on the floor, or ask the kids if they'd like to spend their own money to go out. We've started doing this with our kids, and it's amazing how quickly they decide they don't want to eat out!

5. *It's good to learn from others.* Proverbs 15:22 says, "Plans fail for lack of counsel, but with many advisers, they succeed." If you have stories to share about your experience with money, share them. If you have family members who've been especially wise savers or investors, ask them to spend some time talking with your children. If there's someone in your child's life whom he or she respects, and that person is wise with money, use that influence to speak into your child's life. Look around for resources that will communicate godly biblical truths. These are especially helpful if you as the parent are learning with your children! Also, let your children see you seeking counsel from others on financial decisions. This might include a financial counselor, your pastor, or your spouse.

6. *Money doesn't come from the ATM.* When I would tell my kids, "I don't have money," they'd reply with impatience, "Just go to the ATM and get some." Without guidance, they have no concept that you have to put money into the bank to get money out of the machine. Share the truths about income—how much taxes take out, how much goes to things like debt repayment, bills, and groceries. Show them that while moms and dads want to give things to their kids and do fun activities, we also have to be wise with our money so there'll always be money in that machine. A

note here: Be careful how much you share about hardships; you don't want your child to feel anxious or desperate about your situation. Ask God to help you balance communicating reality and being protective.

7. *Money is best appreciated when spending decisions are placed in kids' own hands.* We've given our kids control over their expenses for the past couple of years and have found that this works quite well for tweens and teens. We were constantly being nickled and dimed over this skating night, that shirt, this movie, that youth event, etc. So we started giving them an allowance, paid each time Curt gets paid. We intentionally gave them enough to cover these types of events. Now when they ask to do something, we can reply, "I don't know, do you have the money?" Most surprising to me is how often they'll decide that an event isn't "worth it" if they have to use "their" money! Additionally, instead of just taking our kids shopping for clothes, we give them the actual money, in cash, that we've budgeted and tell them they can spend it on whatever they want. But when it's gone, it's gone. You should see them checking price tags and working at making their money stretch! Letting our children make their own spending decisions has gone a long way toward teaching them about the value of money.

Recently I overheard a conversation in a restaurant. A woman was lamenting to her friend about how inept her son, a college graduate, was with money. "He completely blew through his whole first paycheck," she explained, speaking loudly in her frustration. "I had to sit down with him and walk him through how to budget his money. I showed him how he needed to deduct for his gas, his insurance, his cell phone bill, the cost of his dog, and *then* spend the rest. Otherwise, he'd just spend it all and expect us to bail him out when he didn't have enough to pay his cell phone bill!" As I listened I felt reinforced in our vital need as parents to communicate about money with our children while we have them in our homes and under our influence.

As parents, we must work ourselves out of a job. We have to take the time to prepare our children for adulthood within the protection of our home. In laying this groundwork, we reduce the risk of someday having an adult child at home, frustrated and broke because he or she can't manage money and has never been required to. In teaching children about money, we are at the same time teaching them to be good spouses, good providers, and good stewards. While this instruction takes a lot of our time on the front end, I'd much rather persevere now than have to make up for lost time later.

The best way you can communicate financial truths to your children is to

+ talk about money, don't shroud it in secrecy;
+ make money management a hands-on experience;
+ live out the principles in your own lives, modeling what you hope they will carry into their futures.

A familiar saying is, "Actions speak louder than words." It's wise to make sure our own financial practices line up with what our children hear us say. Children are much more perceptive than we give them credit for. They can also see through our smoke screens with amazing clarity. They want to see us walk the walk, not just talk the talk.

Here are some tips to use with your children:

1. *Teach children the difference between needs and wants.* Show them how to spend money on needs first, then on wants if there's money left over. This is valuable training for when they're on their own.

2. *Teach them how to bargain shop.* Show them the value of waiting until something is on sale, shopping at consignment stores, or using coupons by requiring them to use their own money for things. One year my friend gave her children their clothing budget in cash instead of just taking them shopping. She told them they could buy whatever they could afford, and she was amazed

at how fast they asked to go to Goodwill to look around. I've found that my daughter loves to shop at a local "teen" consignment store, as she knows money goes much farther there, and she can still have the name brands she loves.

3. *If your child, like most children, is begging for a cell phone, get him or her the base plan and then tell them they'll have to buy any additional services like texting or unlimited minutes.* When my son kept exceeding his limit on minutes, we switched to a prepaid cell phone and made him responsible for buying his minutes up front.

4. *Encourage children to work as soon as they're able.* There's an alarming decline today in the work ethic. Children who were raised to work hard will be the exception and not the rule as this generation comes of age. Work includes requiring chores and doing jobs for friends, neighbors, and family members. It's up to you to decide what jobs are for pay and what jobs kids are to do simply as contributing members of the household. We instill a balance of both in our children.

5. *If your child has a trip or large expense coming up, instead of just forking over the money, encourage him or her to raise money for it.* Both our children went on school trips to Washington, and we required them to raise half the money for it through donations and working. Raising their own funds helps them appreciate how much things cost, as well as the things that are done for them.

6. *Arrange for your children to work with outreach projects to under-privileged people in your city or, if possible, to go on a mission trip.* Our oldest went to an inner city and worked for a week as part of a church mission trip. He still talks about the depths of poverty he witnessed there.

7. *If your child seems to always be out of money, require him or her to keep a spending record, documenting every dime he or she spends.* Require your child to turn in that record as a "ticket" for receiving his or her next allowance. Go over the record log with your

child before he or she gets any more money, and discuss where your child made good choices and where he or she could have made better ones. Help your child add up some of the "little" expenses here and there to show him or her how much money those things really cost.

8. *If your child is older, stop paying for luxuries and require him or her to buy these items instead.* Want to go to dinner with a friend? Great! Do you have the money? Want a milkshake from the drive-through? Great! Did you bring your wallet? You'll find they'll often say "no" to these things when they have to use their money and not yours.

9. *Help your child understand the reality of debt by loaning them money, then requiring them to pay you back with interest.* The next time your child wants something, tell him or her that you'll loan the money, but you've drafted a schedule for the child to pay you back. Let him or her buy the item, play with it, and get tired of it, as kids are likely to do. But still require your child to continue to pay for it, even in spite of tears and begging. This will illustrate the hardship that loans can cause and show your child how quickly a "must have" item is forgotten—long before the debt is paid off.

10. *Have your child open a savings account early in his or her life.* We started an envelope system with our children when they were young. In one envelope was put cash for savings, one was for giving, and one was for spending. The envelopes served as a visual, a way for them actually to see how much money was in each category.

11. *Play board games or read children's books about money management.* Many products found on the market help children understand the value of money and spending, budgeting, etc. Using one could be a monthly event done on the same night as allowances are paid along with some sort of "What would you do?" discussion around the dinner table. Money is a huge part of life—it might as well be a fun part of your family's life!

I find that many parents struggle with wanting to indulge their children—to give them the world on a silver platter. But is that real life? Are you preparing your son to be a provider some day, or your daughter to be a wife who honors her husband with her spending choices? Are you truly caring for them? These are hard questions to ask ourselves, but necessary ones. I know that for the first several years of our oldest child's life, he never left a store without a trinket of some sort. Around the age of two, I noticed that my darling boy had become horribly rotten! It reminded me of Proverbs 30:15, "The leech has two daughters. 'Give! Give!' they cry." I was raising a child who seemed to know only how to hold out his hand for more. And I had unwittingly modeled that behavior to him.

We had to work through that sense of entitlement I had unintentionally fostered in my son. To some degree, we'll always be working through it as he looks around at what the world is screaming at him. It's hard to take a stand against this type of indulgence. Your children certainly aren't going to like it! Nor are they going to thank you for instilling good financial sense in them. There will be days when it will seem much easier to give them what they want and forget the high road altogether. But I want to empower you to parent from a big-picture perspective. To focus on that moment far in the future when your children *will* thank you for helping them avoid the pitfalls their friends have found themselves in.

It's easy to believe that your own financial past has made you an ineffective witness to your children. If you have teens they might, in fact, even say as much to you. You could get caught up in thinking that the mistakes you've made will be what your children most remember and that you don't have a hope of changing their future through your example. But that simply would not be true. There is hope for your future and theirs.

Something that recently happened to Curt affirmed this point for me. He was having lunch at a local restaurant when a man approached him and introduced himself. "You might not remember me, but you coached my son several years ago in football." Curt assured him that he did remember both the man, and the man's son, a boy, who at ten years old had been the quarterback of their team. The man went on, "I just wanted you to know that my son had such a great year that year. He had never really been interested in sports up until then, and after that season with you, he developed a real love for the game of football. He kept playing, and all these years later he's a starting outside linebacker on his high school football team. I wanted you to know what an impact you had on him."

As Curt relayed this story to me, he smiled and said, "I wanted to say, 'But we were 0 and 8 that season!'" It was true. That team was horrible. They never won a game. Their record was pitiful. And yet, a life was changed in the midst of a losing season. The same can happen with the financial legacy you leave. Ultimately, it's not your past record that matters; it's the kind of coach you are.

■ STUDY

Read Deuteronomy 4:9; Psalm 22:30–31; Proverbs 6:20–23; and Hebrews 12:5–11.

■ REFLECT, DISCUSS, PLAN

1. Do you struggle with indulging your children? Has this chapter helped you see some areas you could work on with your children?
2. Do you have a vision for your children's financial futures? Have you communicated this vision to them or will you plan to when they're older?
3. Is money a regular, natural topic of conversation in your home? If not, what practical steps can you take to include it more?

■ TAKE ACTION

Choose one of the teaching tips listed in this chapter that you will implement with your child(ren) this week. Discuss with your spouse how and when you will do so.

Chapter 14

INSPIRING HOPE FOR THE FUTURE

Marybeth

As I parked the car in the grocery store lot, I glanced into the car next to me. Sitting in the driver's side was a woman who looked about my age. I noticed a car seat in the back, and I thought she was just another mom like me about to go grocery shopping. Then I noticed she had her checkbook register open and a piece of paper in her lap, a pinched, pained expression etched on her face. In an instant, I knew what she was doing—she was figuring out how much money she had left to spend on food. My heart went out to her, as I'd been there so many times.

As I walked into the grocery store that day, I prayed. I told God how sad that sight made me, and I asked Him to bless that woman and provide for her. I lamented that I had only enough money to buy groceries for our family and couldn't extend any help to her. How I longed to knock on her car window and surprise her with $100 to buy groceries, telling her that God loved her and cared for her and, most importantly, had not forgotten her. And so I told God all about it and promised Him that, as soon as we were out of debt and in a stable position, I'd make blessing others my life's mission.

I've never forgotten that moment, and I know God hasn't either. That day He ignited in me a strong desire to give. I think that, honestly, we all have that desire down deep within us. It just gets buried under the striving for possessions and the struggle to keep our own heads above water. We get so wrapped up in our own situation that we forget to look around at the situations of others.

I share that moment here because I think giving is the perfect way to close out this book. As we envision a life of financial freedom, we have hope for the future. Not hope that we can buy a lot of stuff, but that we can offer others a hope for the future. By casting a vision of what we can do for others when we have our finances in order, we hope you are challenged to think beyond your own four walls. Just think about it: what would life be like with no debt payments? How much money would be freed up to impact the lives of others? What would it be like to extend help to those in need? How many intangible rewards are found in a life that reflects God's heart in this way?

My friend Karen Ehman and her husband, Todd, are true givers. Karen loves to send packages filled with surprises in the mail. She loves to organize and mobilize people to give to a cause she's become aware of. When you're around Karen and Todd, you get a real sense of what a spirit of giving looks like in action. You see the joy on their faces, hear the passion that spills out of them when they talk about giving. Even greater, that spirit is being handed down to their three children, Mackenzie, Mitchell, and Spencer. Karen told me that their kids will come home after hearing about someone in need and say, "Hey Mom, let's go get a hundred-dollar Wal-Mart card and send it to them anonymously!" Karen recently told me about some decisions they made that's left them unable to give to the degree they once did—and how awful it's been for them to be unable to bless others.

My husband and I have had a history of being very careful with our money. Tithers since accepting Christ—in high school for me, in college for him—we have dug deep into what God's Word says about money. For years we existed on a youth pastor's salary. I stayed home and cared for three children who came along over a six-year span. I remember looking in the newspaper once and noticing that, if our children had been old enough for public school, they would have been granted free lunches, based on my husband's income.

However, as I look back on those days, I am amazed at the ways that God took care of us as we tithed faithfully. We owed no debt except our modest mortgage, with monthly payments of $451, on the home we had purchased through a government low-income loan. We owned only one credit card that was used to make hotel reservations or order products. We paid the full amount off each month. We applied God's principles and they worked! Although we certainly didn't live high on the hog, we were debt-free except for our mortgage.

Fast-forward ten years. My husband left the ministry due to too much time demands on our family. He'd seen too many pastors lose their families while they were busy saving everyone else's! Because Todd knows he is not able to juggle a sixty-plus-hour-a-week job working with people and still devote brain energy to his own clan, he opted for a forty-hour-a-week, time-card-punching factory job that requires nothing of him once he leaves work.

This job enabled us to get ahead on our mortgage. We paid extra each month, even if it was only ten to fifteen dollars. When we were finally in the financial place to purchase our dream home, we sold the house we were living in and had $125,000 equity in our pocket. After twenty years of living very frugally, we felt we deserved to get our dream house. And that is exactly what we found. The place is fabulous. Nearly eight acres of woods with a pond and creek to boot. The home was built by an executive who thought he'd live here forever. It has four bedrooms, three and a half baths, cathedral ceilings with a twenty-one-foot-high stone fireplace, a whirlpool tub . . . you get the picture. We bought it just before the market took a downward turn in our Michigan economy. We actually got it a little below market value based on the SEV. The new mortgage would be just over twice our old one. We had crunched all of the numbers so we knew we could afford it. In fact, the bank actually would have loaned us $50,000 more if we'd wanted them to!

However, once we moved in, we soon discovered that our budget was so tight it squeaked! Propane costs jumped and it cost a pretty penny to heat *those pretty cathedral ceilings. Gasoline prices soared and since we now live fifteen minutes out in the country, we have to drive much more than when we lived in our little town. Our gasoline budget nearly tripled! It only took us about five months to realize we had made a mistake. But we had prayed so hard. We had asked God to shut doors to purchasing this home if He didn't want us to buy it. Every time we did, He flung another door wide open! So we were left puzzled. And heartbroken. Not because we were now attached to this big, new home, but because buying this home had cut into our giving.*

My husband, Todd, has the spiritual gift of giving. I try to have the unspiritual gift of cautioning him. It doesn't work. He has given away large amounts of money and once even my minivan, for crying out loud! Okay, so he didn't actually give it away. He sold it to some sweet penny-pinching friends who had been scrimping and saving for a van and had only $1,000 saved. He sold our van to them for that amount even though the Blue Book price on that like-new van was over four times that price! Living in our dream home has not afforded us the luxury of giving much beyond our normal tithe. No more sending gas or department store gift cards anonymously. No more helping out a friend or relative facing a layoff in our weak Michigan automotive economy. And no more impromptu, fun, family weekend trips to the amusement park or to a campground or beach. All of our money is wrapped up in our home.

So we know what we have to do. Sell the house. Only now it is worth less than what we paid for it. In fact, it has now been on the market for nearly two years while we wait . . . and wait . . . and wait. We believe that God will use this situation in the lives of our children to teach them a few things. First, don't ever buy a home that is at the top end of what you can afford. Because, if you do, you can no longer afford to be generous. And secondly, remember that banks do not take into account that you tithe. On paper, we could easily afford to stay here if we just took the 10 percent of our gross income that we give to God each week and apply it to the mortgage. No way. It is the first thing we pay and we will not stop.

God has taught us many lessons through this and has used our example to caution others. We long now to go back to an average house with an average mortgage and give the excess budget money to those causes we know

God believes in. We want to invest in eternity, not the big earthly home we once thought we wanted and deserved.

In Genesis 22:17–18, God told Abraham that He was blessing him so that he could be a blessing to others. He never intended Abraham to hoard his blessings in some storehouse just in case. He never intended Abraham to squander his blessings on new vineyards, more servants, and extra camels. Instead, He wanted him to start looking around, extending the blessing to others with a "pay it forward" mentality for generations to come. He wants the same from us. Instead of looking around at how we can receive blessings, He wants us to be the blessing for someone else.

Poverty Versus Prosperity

Many of us who've struggled with finances become trapped in a poverty mentality. When you think from a poverty mentality, you say things like, "Oh, I could never give to others. I'd never be able to make ends meet if I did." But when you think from a prosperity mentality, you say things like, "I listen to God's promptings and give even when it doesn't make sense. I've learned that He is always faithful." The problem is, most of us define poverty and prosperity by the world's definitions. But God has some definitions of His own.

To understand God's definitions, we must go back to the origin of prosperity. The garden of Eden is characterized as the picture of perfection and abundance—an abundance of resources, peace, and fellowship with God. When everything around you is overflowing and you lack for nothing, you're experiencing prosperity at its peak. As we walk through the garden in our mind's eye, we're staring at the epitome of wealth, by God's design, with Adam and Eve as the world's wealthiest—and only—citizens.

Fast-forward to after the fall. Pain and work have invaded our perfect picture. We see the former wealthy citizens, Adam and Eve, toiling for hours just to have their meager needs met. We know how they feel firsthand. We have the memory tucked away of what that picture of prosperity looks like, and long for the abundance they once had access to. We see that certain things in our world now stand in opposition to each other, and this has changed the way we view our circumstances. These oppositions include the following:

1. Where once we had *priority*, now we have *panic*. Adam and Eve knew that their first priority was to invest in their relationship with God. In a fallen world, we don't have that priority in place, and we feel the sting of His absence in our lives. This absence leaves us feeling desperate for a replacement—and so we try to fill our hearts with cheap counterfeits, leaving us panicked and stressed much of the time.

2. Where once we had *plans*, now we have *pressure*. Adam and Eve's plans were made by God. They spent their days leisurely doing whatever He required, with no sense of urgency or demand. Now, instead of walking out God's plans for us, we're caught up in the rat race of meeting the demands of many others and feeling a sense of mounting pressure.

3. Where once we had *patience*, now we pursue *pleasure*. Adam and Eve knew to wait on God to meet all their needs. They knew that He would provide because they experienced His provision daily. This was a simple way to live. Because we don't have that perspective, we feel we must provide our own pleasure instead of waiting on God. In the process, we put pleasure ahead of God's agenda and forfeit our character.

4. Where once we had *prayer*, now we have *persecution*. If prayer is simply talking to God, then Adam and Eve had a perfect prayer life. They knew what it meant to commune with their Creator. They had the security of His presence and felt His nearness. Not until Satan entered the picture did they understand what being disconnected from Him really meant. But by then, it was too late. Satan had found his way in between us and God, and he has been persecuting us ever since.

5. Where once we had *promises*, now we have *pride*. Adam and Eve knew firsthand that God keeps His promises. They had witnessed His hand of provision and protection. They reveled in the sound of His voice speaking instruction and encouragement into them. When they found themselves alone, they realized that their pride had caused this break in relationship. In trying to be like Him, they lost Him. Since that day we've battled our own pride, our own desire for control, and let it stand between us and God's promises.

When we walk through the garden of Eden, we see that the true definition of prosperity is fellowship with God. Conversely, the true definition of poverty is being cut off from God. In prosperity, we have all we need, and our souls are peaceful within us. In poverty, we want for everything and our souls are restless, searching for what was lost. As you walk through the garden, never forget that what your soul is really searching for is that lost fellowship with God. Anything else you might try to squeeze in will fall short of that perfection we all long for. And yet, all this searching and longing isn't what God intended for us. It's still possible to experience promises, prayer, patience, plans, and priorities on this side of heaven. Jesus prayed, "Your kingdom come, your will be done *on earth as it is in heaven*" (Matt. 6:10, emphasis mine). He came that we would have life, and have it to the full (John 10:10). He makes it possible for us not to be lacking in anything (James 1:4). We just have to know where to look (Matt. 6:33), and what to hold onto (Deut. 30:20).

Walking in fellowship is being connected to Him and responding to His promptings. The story of the Good Samaritan is a perfect picture of how God desires us to live. We must reflect God's character in our dealings with others, not a character that crosses to the other side of the road—or room—to avoid a person in need. When we reach out to others, we exemplify His character. We honor Him with our lives. We get our hands dirty for Him because He went to the cross for us.

Be a Blessing

We go to a church that isn't afraid to get dirty. Instead of just talking about reaching people, it actually reaches people. I've watched our staff and volunteers venture into parts of our city that very few people would ever go into. Whether building a Habitat home or helping an unwed teenage mom, the very core of our church focus is giving. The biggest example of this giving mind-set happened on a recent Sunday, when our church kicked off its capital campaign by giving money away. As the offering plate was passed, everyone was invited to take out an envelope containing various amounts of money—five, ten, twenty, all the way up to $1,000! Chunks Corbett, the executive pastor, says about that day, "The total given away was the equivalent of the current weekly average of the amount we usually took in. And we didn't take up an offering that day. I remember because it was tight for us that following week."

The people who took the envelopes were instructed to look for ways to bless someone with the money they had received. And they couldn't just give it back to the church. They had to look for people to bless; to pray and ask God to show them who He would have them bless. They invited people to post stories about what they had done with their money on a special Web site. Page after page quickly filled with the blessings that the givers experienced and the ways they were challenged to give all the more.

This project ignited a spirit of giving within our church that has spread far beyond those individuals who received envelopes. Many people wrote to say that they gained such joy from giving that they were inspired to keep doing so with their own money. Families were inspired to pool their money and create family giving projects. People shared how they gave to strangers, people they knew at work, their child's teacher, and even their server at restaurants. And always there was attached to the money a reminder of God's amazing, individual love for us all. I loved that this project took on the life it did and got us all thinking beyond ourselves. Lives are changed when this happens.

Our friends Scott and Denise felt God asking them to give to their church during the church's capital campaign. At the time of the campaign, they had just committed to adopt a little boy from Liberia, and were already struggling to raise funds for his adoption. Yet they knew that if God was asking, He would provide. So they filled out their commitment card and pledged a certain amount over a two-year period. The very next day after they signed the card, an unexpected refund check arrived in the mail. The amount of the check was just enough, in Denise's mind, for the things that their new son would need when he arrived in their home. "In my mother's heart," she says, "I was planning the bed I would buy him and the clothes I could get with that money." So she was shocked when Scott announced that the money should go to the church as their firstfruits offering. "I remember having to make myself not argue with him about it, and just submitted to his leadership—even though I really wanted that amount to go to our son." As promised, they gave the entire amount of the check to their church.

The day after they gave the money away, Scott was called into the conference room at work. There, much to his surprise, his coworkers gave him a surprise shower in honor of the little boy they were adopting. They presented him with a card, and inside the card was a check for exactly $25 less than the amount they'd just given away. God had nearly restored that amount in full! Denise remembers being amazed that He did that for them. And then that night, a coworker who'd been unable to be at the shower presented them with his gift. You guessed it. A gift card for $25! God hadn't just restored a portion of the money they gave away—He had restored it all. Denise says she often reflects on this personal illustration of what giving and trusting and submitting is all about. "I'm not saying that God does that every time," she says, "but more times than not, when we surrender freely, He finds a way to bless us unexpectedly."

If you're not able to give right now because it takes more money than you have just to live, don't let this chapter depress you. I pray that it will inspire and challenge you. That you will be able to take your eyes off your current circumstances and fix them on the hope that awaits you. By committing to do the things we've discussed in this book, you'll eventually be able to give like never before. It will happen. You won't have to wish you could help the lady in the grocery store parking lot, who's wondering how she's going to afford groceries; you'll be able to knock on the window, and press money into her hand, telling her as you do, "God loves you and He wants you to have this today." Don't we all want to know that God is aware of our struggles and is working on our behalf? Wouldn't it be exciting to be a part of that confirmation for someone? Blessing others, I've found, is as much a blessing for us as we learn to listen to God's promptings and respond—knowing in a very real way that He is active on this earth and that He cares for His people.

On the tenth of every month, according to a prayer schedule I use, I pray this verse: "But just as you excel in everything—in faith, in speech, in knowledge, in complete earnestness and in your love for us—see that you also excel in this grace of giving" (2 Cor. 8:7). I ask God to help us to excel in our faith, our speech, our knowledge, our earnestness, and our love for others, and especially to help us excel in giving, as this verse says. I ask Him to pour out a spirit of giving on our family. This monthly prayer reminder is a good time to refocus and challenge myself not to have tunnel vision—to look outside our own circumstances at ways we can minister to the needs of others. More than simply praying for opportunities, I pray for an unquenchable desire for me, Curt, and our children. I pray that we'll have a passion for giving that outweighs a desire for material things. I pray for God's vision and inspiration to seek out creative ways to give.

My friend Ann Voskamp found a way to give above and beyond their family income. As the author of the *A Child's Geography* curriculum, she decided that all the royalties from the sale of these books would go to support World Vision's work around the world.

We're a one-income family, the parents of six children. Thrift-store finds clothe us. Our minivan, bought used, and now over twelve years old, serves us well. We don't own any televisions, DVD players, or iPods. Vacations are simple affairs: camping near home, day trips, canoeing down rivers.

But God's done this thing in us that makes us not want to get more, but give more. And He used this story, a true story that my frugal, God-fearing Dutch mother-in-law once read in a church bulletin and passed on to our family. It's a story we've often read around the dinner table, pulling the crinkled, dog-eared bulletin insert from the family Bible. Every time the children bust with giddy delight. And me, too, through the tear blur.

And so we share with your family the story, "A Rich Family," that changed us.

Eddie Smith was fourteen in 1946, living at home with her two sisters and widowed mother, when her pastor announced four weeks before Easter that a special offering would be collected on Easter Sunday to help a poor family.

The Smith family gathered after church to see how they could best contribute. Though Mother Smith struggled to make ends meet, the girls and mother decided to eat only potatoes for one month, fifty pounds of them, which would tally up a savings of $20 from the grocery bill. And if they didn't listen to the radio for that month, and were careful not to turn on lights unless necessary, the electrical bill, too, would offer savings. The sisters threw themselves into cleaning, yard work, babysitting jobs. They invested in cotton loops to make potholders, three for $1.00. They made sixty potholders and made another $20.

Eddie writes, "That month was one of the best of our lives. Every day we counted the money to see how much we had saved. At night we'd sit in the dark and talk about how the poor family was going to enjoy having the money the church would give them."

The girls had no new clothes for Easter, but they had three crisp $20 bills and one $10 bill in hand for that happy walk to church Easter morning. It was a mile to the church, and it was raining, and there was no umbrella to be had, and Eddie's older sister only had cardboard lining the bottom of her shoes, patching up the holes. But none of that mattered. When that offering plate was passed around, the Smith family, seated second pew from the front, could hardly contain themselves. Each sister put in a $20 bill and Mother the $10 bill. They sang all the way home.

After a celebration dinner of boiled Easter eggs with fried potatoes, a knock came on the Smith front door. It was the minister. With an envelope. Mother spoke a few minutes at the door, then quietly brought the envelope back to the table. Several bills slipped out of the envelope and on to the table: one $10 bill, those three new $20 bills, and a total of seventeen $1 bills. No one spoke.

"We kids had such a happy life that we felt sorry for anyone who didn't have our mom and dad for parents and a house full of brothers and sisters and other kids visiting constantly," writes Eddie. "We thought it was fun to share silverware and see whether we got the spoon or the fork that night. We had two knives that we passed around to whoever needed them. I knew we didn't have a lot of things that other people had, but I'd never thought we were poor. That Easter day I found out we were."

It was a long, quiet week in the Smith house, the realization setting in. Come Sunday, no one was interested in going to church, but Mother insisted. What a different scene from the previous week. The sun shone that mile walk up to services. But the girls didn't talk, no one even joining Mother on the one verse she feebly sang.

The speaker that Sunday was a missionary from Africa, sharing how $100 would roof a church in Africa. The minister urged the congregation to sacrifice to help these poor brothers and sisters in the Lord.

"We looked at each other and smiled for the first time in a week. Mom reached into her purse and pulled out the envelope," recalls Eddie. [And here is where my chin always trembles, voice quavers, and the kids rub their hands with happiness.]

"She passed it to Darlene. Darlene gave it to me, and I handed it to Ocy. Ocy put it in the offering. When the offering was counted, the minister announced that it was a little over $100. The missionary was excited. He hadn't expected such a large offering from our *small church. He said, "You must have some rich people in this church." Suddenly it struck us! We had given $87 of that "little over $100." We were the rich family in the church! Hadn't the missionary said so? From that day on I've never been poor again.*[1]

Eddie's story changed our family. It's true: though we may not have what others have, we aren't poor. One point three billion people with whom we share this planet live on less than a dollar a day.[2] How could we give to those in abject poverty? While we drive our cars and put away the laundry and read stories to the children and serve up the dinner plates, children have died today because of starvation and preventable disease. Couldn't we, too, find ways to sacrifice, to share what we have with those really in need?

God has given us much from which to share, and more than merely financial resources. He's given gifts. Like the Smith girls looping up potholders and offering the sales to the Lord, our family decided to give our talents too. We'd be faithful to using our gifts for His glory, and whatever monies He decided to raise from our projects would be His.

The children began a business making granola cereal. Late nights, they'd press their heads close together and count out the change earned from their sales. Then a voice would pipe up, "How much money again does it take to give a family clean water?" Little collections, day after day, could make a difference. And I followed the children's example; I offered up words. All royalties from a writing project, a geography series for curious kids, were offered to World Vision. If, in writing about global geography, we wanted to answer Christ's great commission to go into all the world, we'd go giving.

And our family has discovered that there really isn't any better way than giving! Scripture declares that it's better to give than to receive (see Acts 20:35), and research confirms it: a study following individuals over a fifty-year span found that those who were giving during high school years experienced better physical and mental health throughout their lives.[3] We wanted that for our children, for us, giving of our resources, our talents, as Jesus calls us to. And knowing His blessings in that. We wanted our faith to have real teeth to it, our children to see that we took God at His Word, that all that we have really is His.

We tried out Malachi 3:10: "'Bring the whole tithe into the storehouse, that there may be food in my house. Test me in this,' says the LORD Almighty, 'and see if I will not throw open the floodgates of heaven and pour out so much blessing that you will not have room enough for it.'" We looked hard at Deuteronomy 15:10: "Give liberally and be ungrudging when you do so, for on this account the LORD your God will bless you in all your work and in all that you undertake" (NRSV).

And we as a family have found what Eddie knew: You can never outgive God. Whatever we give, He will more than match, double, multiply in blessings returned. In Him, we know no poverty, only riches unending.

A Future Built on Hope

Across the Whalen family budget spreadsheet Curt has written the following quote from Dave Ramsey: "Live like no one else so I can live like no one else." As he opens that spreadsheet each day to take out our expenditures and make financial decisions for our family, this is his reminder that we are going against the culture with our decisions. It's not always easy to do. Remember that "for sale" sign in front of our house? Well, it sold after being on the market for nearly a year. Finally we were released to go and find the home of our dreams. We had worked hard to pay off debt and could go and buy the home we "deserved," according to what the world told us. And yet, something kept tugging at us. If we bought the most home we could afford, what would that do to our ability to give, to live securely, to leave breathing room in our budget each month? We had a decision to make. We had to intentionally choose to live like no one else so we could live like no one else.

After weeks of searching and talking, instead of moving on up, we simply moved across. As I write this, we've decided to buy a home in our very same neighborhood. We'll pay only about ten thousand more than the sale price of our old home. This home needs work, but it offers the space our family needs. It doesn't have all the latest niceties we've seen in the various other homes we've looked at. But we've pulled back long enough to ask ourselves, "Do we really need all those extras?" And the answer is, of course, no. We need space, and God has provided that. And as we have the money to do so, we'll add those little extras over time. And we won't be strapped or struggling as we do.

Just before we made this decision, we went to look at "the dream house." This house was beautiful. Situated on a large, wooded one-acre lot, it offered the best of the best in accoutrements—granite countertops, fine hardwood floors, and many custom features. I walked through the house with my mouth hanging open, dabbing at the bit of drool that threatened to roll down my chin. My realtor couldn't contain her excitement and threatened to buy the house if we didn't! A huge screened-in porch covered the back of the house, and I could just picture our family gathered there for barbecues on warm spring nights. Behind the house was a separate, air-conditioned building complete with a personal gym. It took everything in me not to pronounce the house "Sold!" right then and there.

Later that day, Curt came to me with a plan of how we could get that house. We agreed it was a great opportunity to buy what would be our "forever" house. We imagined our grandchildren visiting us there and anticipated years of family memories. It would take some finagling, we agreed, but it would be worth it to own such a beautiful house. We agreed that we wouldn't make an offer right away, but would take some time to think and pray about it.

The very next day, Curt came to me with a realization. "As I began to play with the numbers to get us into that house," he said, "I realized that tithing would be the first thing we'd have to cut out if times got tough." He looked at me with real panic in his eyes. "That's not who we are anymore," he said. "And I don't ever want to be in a position where we can't give." I knew he was right. And I knew that beautiful home would be someone else's beautiful home. As I asked myself, "But will it make me happy?" I had to answer, as always, *no*. I know that house won't make me happy. But being financially secure, being able to do things for my children, and being able to give to others does fill me with joy. No dream home is worth giving up those things. I've learned that happiness is only found when your circumstances are filled with hope. Moving to a house that stretches us too far only pushes hope out of our reach. I don't want to go back to living that way. I'm choosing hope instead.

What does your hope for the future look like? Is it different than when you began this book? Is your vision for the future mired in the muck of materialism? Or is it grasping for the eternal blessings of fellowship with God and participating in His activity? I pray that, as we close this book, we have given you not only the inspiration and encouragement to get out of debt, but the vision and hope for the bright future that awaits you and others when you do. Our prayer is that God has used this book to strengthen your marriage, to get you talking about your money in a productive way, and to have a healthy view of your financial future. We hope we've provided a bridge to take you from where you've been to where you're going. To help you stop being financially frantic and walk in the blessings of being financially free.

■ STUDY

Read the story of the Good Samaritan found in Luke 10:25–37. Then read Luke 6:38; 2 Corinthians 8:1–15; and James 1:27.

■ REFLECT, DISCUSS, PLAN

1. How has this chapter made you think about giving?
2. What is holding you back from giving?

■ TAKE ACTION

Designate a day to pray for your family to have a spirit of giving. Choose a verse from this chapter that speaks to you, and at least once a month pray it aloud.

NOTES

Chapter 1: Finding Hope

1. Pat Regnier and Amanda Gengler, "Men, Women . . . and Money," *CNNMoney.com*, March 14, 2006, http://money.cnn.com/2006/03/10/pf/marriage_short_moneymag_0604/index.htm.

2. Aleksandra Todorova, "The Six Financial Mistakes Couples Make," *SmartMoney*, updated on June 11, 2008, http://www.smartmoney.com/divorce/marriage/index.cfm?story=mistakes.

3. Ben Woolsey and Matt Schulz, "Credit Card Industry Facts, Debt Statistics 2006–2008," Creditcards.com, updated October 22, 2008, http://www.creditcards.com/credit-card-news/credit-card-industry-facts-personal-debt-statistics-1276.php.

4. Jeannine Aversa, "AP-AOL Poll: Debt Hurts Your Body, Too," SF-Gate, June 9, 2008, http://www.sfgate.com/cgi-bin/article.cgi?f=/n/a/2008/06/09/financial/f041255D40.DTL&feed=rss.business.

Chapter 3: Unloading Financial Baggage

1. Gary Chapman, *The Five Love Languages* (Chicago: Northfield, 1995).

2. The framework of pages 38–42 is from Jackie Wellwood, *The Busy Mom's Guide to Simple Living* (Wheaton, IL: Crossway, 1997), 83–89.

3. Jeannine Aversa, "AP-AOL Poll: Debt Hurts Your Body, Too," SF-Gate, June 9, 2008, http://www.sfgate.com/cgi-bin/article.cgi?f=/n/a/2008/06/09/financial/f041255D40.DTL&feed=rss.business.

Chapter 4: Becoming a Team

1. Aleksandra Todorova, "The Six Financial Mistakes Couples Make," *SmartMoney*, updated June 11, 2008, http://www.smartmoney.com/divorce/marriage/index.cfm?story=mistakes.

Chapter 7: Learning to Live on Less

1. Glynnis Whitwer, *Work@home: A Practical Guide for Women Who Want to Work from Home* (Birmingham, AL: New Hope, 2007).

Chapter 9: Facing Unexpected Expenses

1. *The Ryrie Study Bible*, New International Version (Chicago: Moody, 1986), 564.
2. L. B. Cowman, *Streams in the Desert* (Grand Rapids: Zondervan, 1997), 125.
3. Beth Moore, *To Live Is Christ* (Nashville: Broadman and Holman, 2001), 143.

Chapter 12: Replacing Comparison with Contentment

1. Helen H. Lemmel, "Turn Your Eyes Upon Jesus," 1922.

Chapter 13: Building a Financial Legacy

1. Mary Hunt, "Debt Proof Your Kids," *ParentLife*, October 2007, 19.

Chapter 14: Inspiring Hope for the Future

1. Eddie Ogan, "The Rich Family in Church," Mikey's Funnies, http://www.mikeysfunnies.com/archive/richFamily/index.html.
2. Kevin Miller, "Conversations: The Rich Christian," *Christianity Today*, April 28, 2008, http://www.christianitytoday.com/ct/1997/april28/7t5068.html?start=1.
3. Audrey Barrick, "Giving Increases Good Fortune, Happiness," *The Christian Post*, April 8, 2007, http://www.christianpost.com/article/20070408/26759_Giving_Increases_Good_Fortune,_Happiness.htm.

ABOUT THE AUTHORS

Marybeth Whalen is a speaker and contributing writer for Proverbs 31 Ministries. The author of *For the Write Reason*, Marybeth has also written for *ParentLife*, *Money Matters* newsletter, *The Old Schoolhouse*, *Hearts at Home* magazine, and *Homeschooling Today*. She contributes regularly to the daily online devotions of Proverbs 31 Ministries. She and Curt are the parents of six children, which has taught them much about how to stretch a dollar.

Curt Whalen is a trained financial counselor through Crown Financial Concepts. He has years of experience helping couples establish budgets, solve financial problems, and learn to communicate more effectively. He has written articles for *TEACH Magazine* and *Money Matters* newsletter and has contributed to books by authors Lysa TerKeurst and Melanie Chitwood.

Marybeth and Curt want to hear from you! Visit their blog to ask questions and leave comments. They'll post new information about financial issues and current events. They'll share their struggles and celebrate with you as you journey toward financial freedom. They invite you to send your stories of your victories and what God has shown you. Find Marybeth and Curt at www.marybethandcurt.blogspot.com.

ABOUT THE AUTHORS

Are you interested in bringing a "Learning to Live Financially Free" seminar to your church?

Curt and Marybeth would love to come and share the message of this book in a one- or two-day seminar. Using stories, humor, and practical tips designed for today's busy family, the Whalens will encourage couples and equip them to break out of the bondage of debt, establish their financial house on a solid foundation, and enjoy financial freedom.

A great outreach event for your community, these workshops can be designed around the unique needs of your church or organization.

For more information or to make arrangements, contact Curt and Marybeth at www.marybethandcurt.blogspot.com.